"*Thinkin' Drinkin'* i
on a subject domina
discerning as it is bal
"automatic" behavio,
to restrain, but even unwittingly encourage. Drawing on a compelling blend of personal and professional experience, Richard Thatcher addresses the dangers of youthful binge drinking in the context of the benefits of normal, responsible drinking. Dr. Thatcher shows how drinking habits are formed by choices people make in their social environments. In so doing, he empowers readers to substitute good habits for bad habits. The more people read *Thinkin' Drinkin'*, the better for their—and our—safety and well-being."

-- Archie Brodsky, Department of Psychiatry, Harvard Medical School; coauthor of *Love and Addiction* and *The Truth About Addiction and Recovery*

"Dr. Thatcher presents a clear and compelling common sense set of tools, of particular value for young people who want to learn how to drink sensibly. Readers, will benefit from this realistic preventative approach to making reasonable choices and avoiding more serious problems related to drinking alcohol. In a treatment centre setting, clients of any age will benefit from how Dr. Thatcher differentiates problem drinking patterns from alcohol dependency and how he succinctly outlines specific ways to avoid the latter. In a more general and exciting sense, his ideas will inevitably lead to an increased focus on personal responsibility in this area, and the much needed reduction in harms related to drinking alcohol."

-- Michele Ketzmerick, *Director, Saskatchewan Impaired Driver Treatment Centre*.

Thinkin' Drinkin'

From the Teen Years Forward:
A Rational, Safe, Worry-Free Approach to
Lifetime Alcohol Use or Abstinence

Richard W. Thatcher

BALBOA
PRESS
A DIVISION OF HAY HOUSE

Acknowledgements

This book is dedicated to my loving, supportive wife and best friend, who is also an honest but gentle critic of my ideas and writing—and to my oldest (now adult) children, Megan and Carlene, and their mother, Judith, who suffered needlessly from the effects of my stinkin' drinkin' days.

Much of the contents in the book were affirmed by my own experience and some originated in it. In truth, the best ideas in the book were largely derived from the path-finding researchers, counselors, sociologists, social workers and psychologists who have worked so hard and with such courage amidst the resistance of a tenaciously entrenched, received but misguided, wisdom, to finally establish a scientific foundation for a sensible, effective, problem-solving in substance abuse through both self-help and treatment. Some of these path-finders include Martha Sanchez-Craig; Alan Marlatt; L.C. and M.B. Sobell; William Miller; Carlo C. DicClemente; Nick Heather; Ian Robertson; Stanton Peele; and Archie Brodsky.

Copyright © 2011 Richard W. Thatcher

All rights reserved. No part of this book may be used or reproduced by any means, graphic, electronic, or mechanical, including photocopying, recording, taping or by any information storage retrieval system without the written permission of the publisher except in the case of brief quotations embodied in critical articles and reviews.

Balboa Press books may be ordered through booksellers or by contacting:
Balboa Press
A Division of Hay House
1663 Liberty Drive
Bloomington, IN 47403
www.balboapress.com
1-(877) 407-4847

Because of the dynamic nature of the Internet, any web addresses or links contained in this book may have changed since publication and may no longer be valid. The views expressed in this work are solely those of the author and do not necessarily reflect the views of the publisher, and the publisher hereby disclaims any responsibility for them.

The author of this book does not dispense medical advice or prescribe the use of any technique as a form of treatment for physical, emotional, or medical problems without the advice of a physician, either directly or indirectly. The intent of the author is only to offer information of a general nature to help you in your quest for emotional and spiritual well-being. In the event you use any of the information in this book for yourself, which is your constitutional right, the author and the publisher assume no responsibility for your actions.

Any people depicted in stock imagery provided by Thinkstock are models, and such images are being used for illustrative purposes only.
Certain stock imagery © Thinkstock.

ISBN: 978-1-4525-4279-9 (sc)
ISBN: 978-1-4525-4277-5 (hc)
ISBN: 978-1-4525-4278-2 (e)
Library of Congress Control Number: 2011961100

Printed in the United States of America
Balboa Press rev. date: 12/7/2011

Contents

Chapter 1 1
    The Purpose of this Little Book With the Silly Sounding Title

Chapter 2 8
    'No Angel, Me!' Some Thoughts About *My* Stinkin' Drinkin' Past

Chapter 3 22
    The Benefits of Drink

Chapter 4 40
    Volume of Alcohol Consumed and Drunkenness

Chapter 5 47
    The Stinkin' Consequences of Careless Drinking

Chapter 6 67
    Types of Stinkin' Drinkin'

Chapter 7 84
    Being Young, Foolish and 'Getting Wasted'

Chapter 8 99
    Risk Factors for Becoming an Alcoholic

Chapter 9 111
    'Freeze-framing,' then Changing, Automatic Thoughts (The Foundation of the *Thinkin' Drinkin'* Strategy)

Chapter 10 120
    Thinkin'-*Not*-Drinkin' (Liberating Strategies for Alcoholics,
    Potential Alcoholics, and Others Who Simply Shouldn't Drink)

Chapter 11 148
    The Thinkin' Drinkin' Strategy for Potential Problem
    Drinkers (i.e., Most of You)

Chapter 12 175
    A Concrete Strategy for Sensibly (and Safely) Managing a
    Typical Drinking Session

Chapter 13 185
    Reinforcing Thinkin' Drinkin' By Finding More Satisfying
    Alternatives

Chapter 14 197
    Afterward

References 203

Appendix 211

About the Author 215

Chapter 1

The Purpose of this Little Book With the Silly Sounding Title

---

This book has been prepared for *you* if you are a teenager or young adult who thinks that getting "wasted" on booze is a hoot—and getting drunk is a "blast."

If you are in the same age group and you think that spending time with friends on a regular basis while "getting into the sauce" but just getting a little "tipsy" might become part of your lifestyle, then the book is also for you.

The book is also offered up to those of you who haven't yet given much thought to how you should approach drinking – probably most of you -- but, when the subject comes up, you recognize that it probably makes sense to give the matter some serious attention.

In North America, social scientists now apply the terms "youth" and even "adolescence" to not only teens but to anyone who falls between the early teens and the early thirties. The reasoning is that, for most young people in the United States and Canada today, the road to self-support is much longer than the one their parents travelled. In fact, this change has spawned a new term, specifically, "emerging adulthood." The term — emerging adulthood — has been coined in response to the extended length of time it now takes to settle into a full-time occupation, establish a career, and sever financial and residential dependency on parents; it refers to those of you in the early twenties to early or even mid-thirties.

So, in terms of age, my target group is pretty wide-ranging. It includes the "emerging adult." I do expect, however, that the age range of my most common readership is going to fall between fifteen and twenty-four years old—and for the younger segment of that range, the book's contents will most often be passed on through searching parents, concerned teachers, substance abuse educators, guidance counsellors, and, occasionally, by friends who are avid readers in general.

I also recognize that people do start drinking at many different ages and, for this reason, the book is intended for *all* age groups with members who are now or will soon be confronted with critical decisions about the nature and quality of their own drinking practices.

The book is also for youth of all sexual orientations, including females, males, bisexuals, gays, lesbians, the transgendered, and the "rainbow vanguard," by which I refer to the most sexually open-minded of young people. Drinking to excess is all too often an escape from the pain and complications caused by the prejudice of mainstream sexuality. Those with an alternative lifestyle of intimacy have every reason to carefully consider how drinking fits into their lives.

Our society has come a long way in gaining a civilized understanding of alternative expressions of sexuality but it has a very long way to go and, on that path, cruelty remains a very familiar part of life for gays, lesbians and transsexuals—even for those with bisexual preferences. The psychological burdens of being stigmatized, experiencing painful comments and, sometimes, bullying, can lead to an overwhelming sense of isolation. In reaction to that marginalization members of sexual minorities are often tempted to turn to overly frequent drinking patterns or drinking binges as an escape. Unfortunately, both are unhealthy choices and, at times, very dangerous forms of relief, leading to alcohol dependency or unfortunate, even tragic, incidents. So, if you are a member of one of these minorities, having a solid handle on your drinking practices is extremely important, maybe even a life saver.

In the book, I don't give special emphasis to sexual minorities but it will become obvious as you read on that the background material and the sensible drinking (or abstinence) strategies described in the book apply equally to you. It is left to each of you to personalize both your reflections on the various topics covered and your own adoption and modification of the strategies proposed to meet your distinctive, personal needs.

The Growth of Female Drinking

It is also worth noting that getting drunk during adolescence used to be far more common for males than females. That situation has apparently changed substantially in recent years. A study published in September 2001 by the Society for the Study of Addiction to Alcohol and Other Drugs surveyed college and university students under age 25 years old in the United States and Canada.[1] The researchers, who were on the faculty of several prestigious American and Canadian universities, including Harvard, found that girls were even *more* likely than their male counterparts to be current drinkers and they were almost as likely as males to report having participated in heavy drinking episodes. The researchers also found that,

- the average age at which youth in America first try alcohol is 11 years for boys and 13 years for girls.

- By age fourteen, 41% of American children have had at least one alcoholic drink (mass [communion] wine excluded).

- Americans tend to start drinking in their mid-teens–at least they begin to experiment with drinking. In fact, the average age at which Americans begin drinking regularly is 15.9 years old.

More recent data published by the American Substance Abuse and Mental Health Services Administration indicates that approximately one-quarter of Americans aged 12 and over report having engaged in binge drinking in the past month, including 8.8 percent of drinkers in the under-aged, 12-17 year old cohort.

---

[1] The study, entitled "More Canadian Students Drink but America Students Drink More: Comparing College Alcohol Use in Two Countries," included data on both male and female under-25 year old post-secondary students in both countries. The study was published in the September issue of the journal *Addiction* and was carried out by Meichum Kuo, Edward M. Adlaf, Hang Lee, Louis Gliksman, André Demers and Henry Wechsler.

Maybe the book is not for everyone ... well, maybe?

The book may not be for everyone. If you already manage your drinking wisely or if you have a firm, unwavering commitment to abstinence (a resolve to not drink at all, a "teetotaller," as the saying goes), then you won't find the book to be especially useful.

On second thought, even if you are a committed non-drinker, you might find that the information between these covers will help you scratch an enduring curiosity itch about the matter. As a result, it might provide useful information to support your non-drinking decision or it might convince you to waver slightly by drinking on occasions but doing so in a sensible fashion.

> **There is nothing inherently evil about drinking beverage alcohol. It really should be considered with an open mind.**

There is nothing inherently evil about drinking beverage alcohol. It really should be considered with an open mind. My life experience tells me that when people rigidly and without question adopt a and steadfastly adhere to a particular behaviour over many years of their lives, they tend become closed in their thinking about many things—and often less than sympathetic with people who think and act differently than themselves.

Whether you are a drinker or a non-drinker, the information in these pages might also assist you in helping friends to think through how they should approach drinking.

I must also add that, if you are already a sensible, moderate drinker, reading this book should reinforce and further refine your rationale for the approach to alcohol that you have chosen. The book should help you give shape to your personal approach to drinking. It advises you to establish some clearly defined goals and, subsequently, to figure out how you can best achieve them.

I want you to figure out how to manage your drinking in a reasonable way. I see **safety and well-being** as key components of what can justifiably be considered "reasonable" in this matter. I'm referring to *both* your own safety and well-being and the safety and well-being of other people you are in contact with, both during and immediately after a heavy drinking episode.

I also see *good taste, civility* and *fun* as rightful aspects of reasonable drinking.

A Few Words About the Silly Sounding Title

I know the title of this book sounds silly but there was method to my selection. I chose the *Thinkin' Drinkin'* title (in the South of the United States it might be pronounced "Thankin' Drankin'") to grab your attention and, yes, to irritate you just a little. Commercial advertising executives call phrases of this sort "ear worms"—annoying phrases or musical sounds that you find difficult to purge from your memory traces.

Admittedly, the "cutesy" sound of the title would annoy me if I saw it gracing the cover of a book written by someone else, but it would certainly catch my eye. But I *wanted* the title to bug you, to grate on your nerves a little bit. That way, an awareness of the book and, hopefully, its contents, will stay with you, hopefully, for a very long time. I want the concept of *thinkin' drinkin'* to have what a marketing executive would call "brand familiarity."

By the way, the meaning of the title is the opposite of what I call "stinkin' drinkin'," a phrase which, quite deliberately, also has an annoying ring to it. In writing this book, spelling out the difference between these opposites was my preoccupation.

Most People Can *Choose* to be Thinkin' Drinkers

I believe that, compared with other types of drinking problems, there is far too much attention paid to what is often referred to as "alcoholism." Alcoholism is a very real and tragic problem, yet it is but the type of the iceberg when it comes to problem drinking.

I'll discuss the meaning of the term "alcoholism" later in the book and, in fact, I will directly address the problem. By alcoholism I mean *alcohol addiction*: an overwhelming compulsion to frequently and regularly drink alcohol to the point of at least mild intoxication. Intoxication from beverage alcohol results in enormous individual, social and economic costs but only some of that intoxication is experienced by alcoholics.

Compared with the number of alcoholics in the population, there are a whole lot more North Americans whom, on occasion, drink too much. When taken together, the harmful results of the occasional binges in the general population is actually far more costly than alcoholism itself.

Personally, **I advocate drinking** as an enjoyable human recreation, although there is one caveat: I want you to learn how to enjoy it and get the most out of it, with the fewest negative consequences. But I repeat: I do firmly believe that most of you can drink and enjoy it for what it has to offer.

> I'm a great advocate of drinking. It really does have much to offer.

I also firmly believe that **most of you can drink sensibly**, although there are some people for whom drinking is simply an invitation to disaster Some of you may have a biological and/or psychological predisposition to alcohol dependency or to destructive behaviour when you drink. But you can learn to abstain without losing out on anything! Honest! The good things that accompany drinking can all be obtained *without* alcohol.

What I will be arguing may throw you off a little—at least at first read. It will seem like I am a champion of drinking, a don't-give-a-damn blowhard, maybe the devil incarnate. And for most people, who needs to be persuaded to drink? But stay with me. Before you write me off as being irresponsible and lacking sense, give me a little rope and read on to get my full reasoning.

Messages That Simply Try to Scare You Off Drinking Don't Seem to Work!

It is also worth noting that new evidence suggests that the conventional public anti-binge drinking ads aimed at scaring you away from the practice can be counterproductive. Such "anti-drinking" or "responsible" drinking campaigns have long been a mainstay of health departments and health-promoting non-profit organizations.

Unfortunately for both the youth who are being targeted by these messages and taxpayers and charitable contributors who finance such messages, the ads don't seem to be very effective.

In America, as opposed to Europe and many other countries around the world, we tend to view the generous consumption of alcohol as a forbidden fruit for which temporary exemptions are only given for special circumstances, including being "young and wild." Our history has included a strong "temperance" element, driven by strong-minded moralists obsessed with the view that alcohol is a principal cause of individual downfall and family destruction.

The North American perspective has served to sensationalize the drinking experience. Individually, we treat a drunken state as an excuse to express our emotions in extreme ways, whether through angry or soppy, sentimental verbalization, exaggerated body gestures, raw candour and outright belligerence. By generally repressing the use of beverage alcohol – or at least being preoccupied with limiting it — and perceiving its place in society as an extraordinary, contradictory, love-hate, cultural practice, North Americans have unwillingly created a drinking atmosphere that encourages drunkenness, a state that is deemed to promise an attractive, if naughty mix of intense pleasure, low rent adventure that carries with it the potential for very, very high risk.

In fact, the cultural practice of beverage alcohol use is not especially harmful when consumption is treated as a casual, routine part of life and it is not covered with a veil of moral disapproval. Evidence from other societies confirms this. The fact is that the harm in drinking occurs when we take more than our host, physiological systems, including our brains, can easily absorb. There is a safety/harm threshold to almost anything, including even the greatest of pleasures.

> **Note: If you are a *very* impatient reader, start with Chapter 9. That's where a concrete description of the sensible drinking strategies starts.**

Chapter 2

'No Angel, Me!' Some Thoughts About *My* Stinkin' Drinkin' Past

---

You should know that, in my younger years, when it came to drinking, I was no angel. Believe me!

The truth is I had many enjoyable times when I drank, even when I drank to the point of intoxication. Eventually, however, on balance, I came to appreciate that the negative side of my drinking equation overwhelmed its opposite, namely the enjoyable and fun side of the balancing scale. In fact, what convinced me to write this book was the fact that there were all too many incidents of truly regrettable experience when I drank too much.

You could say that the very exercise of writing this book was, at least in part, an act of personal penance delivered dutifully to the righteous demands of my better self, as well as an apology for those many people who were negatively impacted by my drinking.

I am still smarting and sheepish about my early drinking experience. I did enjoy many occasions when I enjoyed the circumstances and tastes of some excellent libations and, on occasion, I still do. I look back with considerable appreciation on so many of those times and tastes in which I partook of wines, beer and John Barleycorn. Yet all too often I stayed for that extra few and, thus, so much of my drinking life was a "downer," as we used to say in the 1960s with galling repetition , and I truly wish that that my to repetitive visitations to that down side *never* occurred.

Even today, after several decades of distance from my heavy drinking years, the unpleasant circumstances and feelings that accompanied or followed my liquid adventures remain a source of considerable psychic discomfort.

On occasion, when trying to get to sleep at night, I still do my *shouldn'tas, why'd I do its* and my *woulda's, shoulda's, coulda's* in my brain while my right fist smashes the pillow in futility. Yes, I still harbour a good deal of profound regret that clearly originates in a long list of badly handled drinking episodes.

When I was in my adolescence, I clearly remember the phrase, "We got 'stinkin' drunk!" It seemed a pretty accurate, concise description of the experience itself. The phrase was also code for a little pride, at least sometimes. We were intent on getting drunk and if it worked out, I think we thought we had actually accomplished something.

But really, what did we accomplish? I'm still not sure. I know we did succeed in just having fun, enjoying each other's company. Not such a bad outcome when you think about it.

Maybe we got a little closer to someone or even intimate with a desirable partner: also a satisfying achievement: clearly nothing to scoff at.

Maybe we got a heavy load of sadness, hurt feelings, anxiety or anger off our chests, or maybe we just filled a temporary void of activity.

I have to be honest in this matter. Having a few drinks is a pretty sure and easy way to relax, break the ice and feel more sociable.

Obviously, there is also the other side of the coin, however. My drinking and the drinking of my friends often simply went too far. In the throes of our drunkenness we could also have easily been injured or killed, done the same to other people, delivered insults to others that we would later regret, or made unwanted babies. We threw the liquid dice with reckless abandon.

In my days at university, our beer drinking sessions were centred on discussions of how to change the world. Often we thought we had it figured out: solving the world's problems, that is. Surprise, surprise, we failed every time.

Often, drunkenness is treated as an excuse for certain kinds of difficult, emotional communications that we find difficult to undertake when we are sober. Admittedly, it works; at least it works occasionally and, in general, at least in some modest measure. But on sober reflection, I think you'll find that you don't need the alcohol to achieve any of the things you expect those bouts of heavy drinking to do for you. In the latter pages of the book I will suggest some of these alternatives—things to do that don't involve using alcohol to modify your mood and enhance your self-confidence.

The Psychology of 'Chasing' in Gambling is Similar to the Compulsion to Repeat the Good Times You've Had When Drinking

> Sometimes heavy drinking sessions are great: exciting and lots of fun. But the outcomes are really like a game of chance. The potential outcomes are stacked against you. With rare exceptions, the more you gamble or the more you drink, the more you lose—and sometimes those losses can be very, very substantial.

If you already have a few years of drinking under your belt, ask yourself how many times your drinking episodes really turned out to be uneventful or not much fun, simply leaving you a little bit (or a great deal) sick the next day. You should also ask yourself what your win-loss ratio looks like. You know, how often over time your expectations of a great drunk have actually been met. I think you'll find that Mistress Alcohol is a very unreliable date.

When I reflect back upon my teen and young adult years, heavy drinking shares something that is central to the dynamics of casino gambling.

While most gamblers occasionally win more than they pay out, over time, the "house," as they say (i.e., the casino), typically takes far more from the gamblers' wallets than what the gambler gains on those few successful outings. In other words, the cumulative balance for the gambler is typically a deficit, well into the red column. For the vast majority of gamblers, the odd battle is won but, ultimately, the war is a significant loss and, occasionally, a disastrous one. Think of the gambler who finally puts up his house in a poker game, loses, and has to deliver the message to his dependent family.

Psychologists who have studied gambling refer to this compulsion to return to gamble again to make up for previous losses as "chasing." The concept is even reflected in screening questionnaires constructed to determine if one is or is not a compulsive gambler, as well as the intensity of that compulsion.

In fact, it is the predictably high gains of the gambling industry, based on the knowledge that most gamblers will lose but will return to recoup their losses, that is the very foundation of its profitability. The compulsion for the gambler to return to play, despite the well-known advantage of the house, is the hope that maybe, just maybe, the next round of gaming might result in the rebalancing of one's win-loss ratio.

It is my contention that heavy drinking works on the drinker in a similar fashion as the chasing dynamic in problem gambling.

The heavy drinker keeps returning to his (or her) indulgence in the hope that he will repeat the good times, the fun conversation late into the night, the striking of new friendships, and/or the completion of the night with intimate relations with a drinking partner of compatible sexual preferences. Those satisfactions are rarely repeated, however, despite the continuing, hopeful returns to the bar. But the drinker keeps coming back, banking on a fading promise. "Maybe . . . just maybe, everything will work out tonight," he says to himself.

> **Heavy drinking sessions work on the individual like casino gambling. You have a few satisfying nights of earnings or sheer fun and time and time again you try and usually fail to repeat that night of success. Pathetically, you keep chasing the good memory without counting your considerable losses.**

It is also my contention that this compulsion to return to achieve the expectations embedded in the brain by those rare, satisfying events is a main driver for the sales of alcohol, just as "chasing" is a main driver of the gambling industry.

The good times associated with a drinking binge tends to stand out in the memory, while the bad nights serve as motivators to try, try and try again to recapture the elusive pleasures of the good nights and the good times. But like gambling, those wonderful nights rarely recur and the balance shifts deeply into the negative results column with the continuation of a lifestyle of heavy drinking.

In both gambling and drinking, a destructive habit can form and a hard-to-overcome addiction can follow. It is a slippery slope, this heavy drinking stuff—and it is always a high risk gamble.

Like the gambler who loses his family home, you can experience enormous losses if you drink too much on even a single occasion. You know what many of those potential losses are. If you haven't given it much thought I'll update you in Chapters 5 and 7 below.

My Personal 'Chasing'

When I say that my pattern of drinking was often idiotic, I'm not kidding. It was nuts! It was fun, a great deal of fun, on a few occasions, and it was that enjoyment that seemed to preoccupy my thoughts rather than the down times. This distorted thought pattern suggested that, despite the many not so good or terrible times when drinking was involved, binge drinking could and hopefully would usher in a helluva good time. The reality reflected in my actual win-loss drinking tallies told a much different story, however.

> **For every one truly satisfying heavy drinking episode, I think I experienced ten or more generally negative experiences.**

Again, looking back and reflecting, I now see that even the good times when I drank tended to yield a significant legacy of regrets: memories of words exchanged or behaviour enacted that was injurious to either myself or other people with whom I had contact during a drinking episode. And studying, working or even enjoying recreational activity the next day was often crippled by a dose of mild nausea or an outright hangover from the overload of a toxic substance in my system.

Worry or regret about what I said or did while drinking the night before was a typical presence the day after a bout of heavy drinking—and sometimes for many days after. When I finally came to do some honest accounting, I had to confront the fact that my win/loss heavy drinking ratio was overwhelmingly in favour of the loss side of the ledger. Obviously, one's memory doesn't allow for any great precision in these matters but when I tried to do a loose, retroactive count, I estimated that, for every one modestly satisfying heavy drinking episode, there were ten or more generally negative experiences. Hardly a great nugget of information for a marketing campaign for heavy drinking!

Personal Costs and Costs to Others: A Sampling of My Own Regrets

There was no clear pattern to my drinking. There was no evidence of a gradual, upward curve mapping a progressive increase in the frequency or amount I drank. Nor was there a gradual intensification of dumb and risky behaviour while I drank. Both of these patterns might have been predicted from the received professional wisdom of the day.

While a predictable, alcohol pattern to my drinking was not in evidence, when I finally gave a serious look back at my drinking behaviour, however, I was embarrassed, full of shame, and very angry at myself. I now wish, so very, very much, that when I was young I had stopped to reflect carefully on my boozing and that, out of that examination, came a thoughtful approach to my use of alcohol.

The drinking style I established in my late teen and young adult years lingered on for a couple of decades into my adult life, although its frequency and intensity waned over time. In those years, careless drinking negatively affected several of the most significant roles in my life: the roles of friend, acquaintance, employee, and later husband and parent. Its impact was expressed in a variety of toxic ways; it directly resulted in some problems and, just as significant, it masked others, thus enabling my avoidance of several central issues in my life. Those very issues deserved and sometimes virtually demanded my full and serious attention.

Some of the costs that I incurred as a result of unmanaged drinking activity included the following:

- **Drinking as an expensive way to overcome my shyness and lack of social self-confidence**

I failed to overcome a crippling sense of shyness during my younger years. I now attribute much of that failure to the fact that I used alcohol as my crutch for overcoming that problem. I used the "tipsy drinker" role as a means of confidently navigating through conversations at social gatherings, overcoming my exceptional sensitivity to humorous jibes (which I came to give back in spades when I was tight), overcoming self-consciousness on the dance floor and, yes, "chasin' da' goils." Unfortunately, the confidence I seemed to gain after having a few drinks did not transfer back to my sober state. There was no learning and thus no ultimate advantage. I learned that the self-confidence gained when drinking does not transfer back to the sober world, so the hope of its transformative potential is misplaced. The real challenge is to learn to conquer a personal trait that we regard as a shortcoming when we're sober—and to learn the interpersonal communication skills to make us comfortable in even our most dreaded social setting.

- **Embarrassment and guilt after a drinking episode: a personal price**

One of the continuing downsides of heavy drinking episodes is feeling embarrassed or ashamed about the exaggerated expression we give to our emotion when we imbibe. Drinking often brings out the meanest of intentions in us. That meanness is typically directed at other people but we can also be pretty hard on ourselves and we set ourselves up for the jests of others. I remember that on far too many occasions I was downright sarcastic, confrontational or just plain mean with other people. I remember so very often making a fool of myself by virtually inviting insults with inappropriate statements or insulting body language.

There were so many days after parties or bar visits that I felt guilty or angry at myself for saying things to people that I later came to deeply regret. Drinking impairment tends to create tunnel vision: we focus on one thing at a time. We get locked into a psychic space that seems to ignore thoughtful reasoning, respect for boundaries and, in general, sensitivity to the needs and feelings of others. We also tend to pay far too little attention to potential consequences for both our actions and words. We talk too much about others and often betray confidences that we would never do if we were sober.

Sometimes we get overly sentimental or whiney when we drink too much. In short, we make bloody fools of ourselves. You remember some of those situations throughout your life.

An episodic, binge drinker acquires many demons and suppresses them as a psychological defence mechanism. However, rather than directly addressing either the drinking problem or the deficiencies that enable the drinking, the problem drinker tends to ignore the root problem, pushing the regrets aside as best s/he can and, in the process, becomes increasingly uncomfortable in his or her own psychological skin. This certainly happened to me, and for far too many years. When my memory returns me to that early, obnoxious behaviour, despite robust attempts, I can't just wish it away.

- **Making bad choices regarding people to hang out with (Mates we only see when we drink are rarely *real* friends)**

I used drinking activity as a context for a good deal of socializing in my late teen and young adult years. For many years, I thought of my drinking partners as friends, only to find years later that, once the heavy drinking was over, those friendship ties diminished or lapsed, most, eventually, being broken off completely. The sarcasm, conflict and behavioural excesses that was accepted, even promoted, during drinking sessions actually left a bad aftertaste during our sober hours. When I quit any excessive drinking, I found that bitter aftertaste stayed with me. I found that friendships born and sustained in heavy drinking bouts are usually not friendships at all.

- **Placing myself and others at great risk**

When I was in my teens and early to late twenties, I placed myself and others at great risk when I drank. For one thing, I got into a lot of confrontations and fights. But the worst of these circumstances involved the times that I drove a car during or shortly after a drinking bout. When I was sober, I was fully cognizant of the stupidity of driving and drinking but when I wanted to drink or when I was drinking, my good conscience went on strike, and I drove. In those years, it was pretty commonplace. In fact, it was the very stupidity of our behaviour in those days that led to the far more rigorous driving and drinking laws of today. Dare I say that drinking and driving was almost normal. It was nuts. My friends and drinking acquaintances all did it and we were all passengers in each other's cars when a drinking driver had hands on the steering wheel. It all seems insane now. I can only say that I'm damned lucky not to have been critically wounded or dead one.

- **Diminishing the quality of family relations**

My drinking drove a wedge between myself and my parents and distanced me from my brother and sister. Because my father was pretty loose with the bottle himself well into his forties, I think maybe I thought it was acceptable to get smashed when I felt like it. For all his foibles, my father was a pretty good guy and he wished the best for his kids. Maybe it was at least partly because I liked and, for the most part, respected him, that I thought that following his lead in matters of the bottle was not such a bad way to go.

My mother was pretty squeamish about the very idea of me drinking at all. In looking back, I think it scared the hell out of her. In fact much of what my brother and I did made her nervous. She grew up in a female dominated household with a very proper English mother and a single, fragile sister with a host of serious health problems. Her father – and my maternal grandfather — was a finishing carpenter who was a sensitive, kind man, someone you couldn't help but regard as a natural gentleman, despite the humbleness of his station in life and the modesty of his income. But Grandpa let his wife rule the home roost and spend most of the parental time available with the girls. So a familiarity with the ways and wiles of boys was thus not much a part of my mother's experience. So the craziness of ordinary adolescent wildness was very foreign to my mother.

As I look back, I can see that not wanting to create more turbulence in my father's life and not wanting to scare my nervous mother, propelled me to find various ways to hide from them almost the entirety of my social life, but especially my drinking. Essentially I began to live what amounted to a double life. Different parts of my life became compartmentalized. My activities during my drinking bouts were something that I simply didn't want my parents to know about. Nor did I want my teachers, other authority figures or even many of my friends and acquaintances to know about my wildest drinking adventures. I tried to keep most of them from those who thought less of people who were heavy drinkers.

Many of my antics during drinking episodes would have scared the hell out of my parents–and, on occasion, they did, like the time I came home bloodied from a scrap with a drunken acquaintance. Like the time one cold and blizzardy New Year's Eve when I took a hitch-hiking trip hundreds of miles to another city after driving my father's old half-ton into a snow bank in the ditch. I went missing for a couple of days as a result and drove my parents crazy with fear. I still shake my head and ask myself in wonder: "What the hell was I was thinking?"

When young North Americans enter adolescence, they typically enter a youth-oriented world that is very much separated from the one occupied by the daily routines and life preoccupations of their parents. Yet when booze becomes a central part of their recreation, communication with parents about their private life often breaks down completely. Sadly, it is very hard to fully recover those innocent and once close bonds after several years of such intense secrecy. In my opinion, there is also, very often, considerable guilt associated with that separation.

> One cold, blizzardy and drunken New Year's eve I drove my father's old half-ton truck into a snow bank and then took off. I hitch-hiked a couple of hundred miles on my way to another city.

Heavy drinking and the wretched hangovers that typically follow rob us of quality time with people we care about, including our kids, once we establish a family of our own. Often, my drinking, which began during my adolescence and proceeded into my adult years, ate into the time that should have been devoted to my responsibilities as a parent and friend to my wife and children. In a typical drinking binge, one's time away from one's family is compounded the next day by the crankiness and basic performance limitations associated with a hangover.

I truly believe that the pattern I have just described is a common one for drinkers who do not develop a clear set of principles to guide their drinking behaviour.

- **Financial costs**

Heavy drinking on a frequent basis is also very costly for your wallet. Beer, wine and spirits are not cheap. The more you drink the emptier your wallet—and the less time you have to sensibly prepare and work from a budget. For the most part, frequent, heavy drinkers lose a lot of money and that money is unaccounted for. I did. I still have no idea how much money I wasted on buying drinks for myself and rounds for others during my many years of drinking. Consider the cost of one night at the bar and you get an idea of just how much you can spend over twenty years.

- **Limiting the potential intrinsic to my talents**

Unmanaged drinking behaviour also forestalled much of the important work that could have flowed from my personal aptitudes, those special gifts that each of us, in distinctive packages, are bestowed with by nature, early nurture, and our own creative application of both. There are so many things I could have accomplished, so much that I could have done for my intimates and children and for other people, so many experiences of a positive nature that I could have enjoyed, if only I thought rationally about my drinking and if I acted on that thinking. Because of my dumb drinking patterns, I squandered far too much of the time available to pursue opportunities that lay before me for personal development and productivity. There were so many things that I now do that were put off because of my drinking and so many goals that will never be fulfilled because of lost time.

You've all heard the phrase, "a wasted youth." I am *very* familiar with what that statement implies. While I think I did accomplish a good deal when I was young, if bouts of heavy drinking were not a significant part of my life, there is so much more that I could have achieved.

Nowhere to Turn

Despite my "crazy drinking ways," which I now look back upon with embarrassment, even shame, nobody or at least very few people, ever really spoke to me with concern about the problem, other than making the odd, confrontational comment. The way those latter comments were delivered just made me mad and I rejected them out of hand.

No one said to me that my drinking style was very dangerous. No one said what I really needed to hear: "If you're going to drink, there are actually sensible ways to do it. You've got to learn to manage it, make it a happy, healthy and safe activity."

Oh it's true that my intimate partners would talk about my problem drinking, but that was only when we were bickering and the words exchanged seemed so obviously biased by the cut and thrust of the immediate wrangle. In addition, their comments were suspect because, at least for a time, they joined in my wild drinking with enthusiasm.

> **During my dumb drinking days, at least when I was in my teens and early twenties, no one was there to confront me in a firm but respectful and caring way, to talk things through, to give me advice, to help me learn to drink sensibly . This book is my attempt to fill the vacuum for those of you who don't have that caring someone to turn to.**

Bouts of heavy drinking are partly thrill-seeking episodes and thrill-seeking is high risk activity. If you ask any highly successful athlete in an extreme sport, the entire experience is about managing the attendant risks in play in order to reduce the probability of injurious outcomes. I remember a former middleweight boxing champion tell an interviewer that he himself always fought in a way to avoid getting hit and that his skills were specific to the ring. He said that he wouldn't even want to try barroom fighting, where there were no rules and he had no experience. From this perspective, the basic orienting principles behind stinkin' drinkin' would never make it as a serious approach to a competitive sport.

Despite the destructive effects of my drinking pattern, which began in an exploratory way in my early teens and gained considerable momentum in my mid-teen years, the only people who spoke with an apparent voice of authority about the matter were those who advised abstinence as the only approach to drinking problems. It is true that there were a variety of contested theories about why people had trouble with drinking. As a person with an academic bent, I explored all that reading. I don't know what all that problem drinking-as-pathology talk and reading did to me, other than make me think it was gobbledy gook or something to run from. Somehow my reading of the available literature on the subject just either scared me off or made me sceptical about the validity of the material.

When I was young, the only practical advice available in the form of reading material at the time essentially said the same thing: "If you're having problems with your drinking, then don't drink at all! Some went so far as to say drinking was intrinsically evil; it is a destructive force, they said, to be avoided like the plague. In response to the teetotalling advice that was so widely and freely available, I can remember thinking that it was easy for them to say, but almost everyone I knew and wanted to spend time with socialized at bars or at parties. In both venues, drinking was the main dish on the evening's menu of activities.

In the end, I 'got off lucky,' compared to so many others.

Despite my many and deep regrets about foolish drinking episodes, I got off lucky. The impact of badly managed drinking on my life has been enormous and many are my regrets about not nipping it in the bud when I was very young. Some of those regrets are huge, continuing to occupy seemingly closed departments of my memory that release themselves in unpredictable patches of unwelcome reverie. Yet the demons that haunt my psyche that were born in my drinking years are minuscule compared to those of so many others. There are so very many people who have done things when intoxicated that have ruined their own careers or the careers of others, destroyed their own reputations or the reputation of others, or injured, maimed or even killed themselves or others. Obviously, compared with those people, I have been very, very lucky.

Chapter 3

The Benefits of Drink

Beverage alcohol has been around for a long, long time and, as my favourite barber recently observed, "It ain't goin' away anytime soon!"

In fact, alcohol has been a significant element of the world's cultural landscape for thousands of years. A part of human endeavour since before the dawn of written history, beverage alcohol is thought by some scholars to be our oldest mood-modifying drug. There is little doubt that it is at least to be counted among the earliest of such substances.

Compared with other drugs, alcohol is also, almost certainly, the "buzz trigger" that spans the recreational consumption habits of the largest number of human cultures and traverses the widest span of human geography.

With all that inclusion in human affairs, surely drinking beer, wine and spirits yields some benefits–and it does, despite those strident finger wagers who simply see beverage alcohol as a devilish genie, capped in a bottle.

With no apologies forthcoming, I offer a robust tip of my glass to good beer, wine and liquor: "Here's to you!"

And join me in another toast to alcohol that utters the salutation: "Here's to a sensible relationship in which I am in control."

Types of Alcoholic Beverages

Some historians have argued that early human beings learned to use alcohol as a beverage after watching animals eat fermented fruits lying on the ground in the forest.

Whatever the original thought processes that led to the conscious production of beverage alcohol, several pre-literate human societies discovered it long ago. They found out that if you crushed certain forms of fruit and allowed them to stand for a period of time in a container, a process called *fermentation* would occur that would produce alcohol.

The question of *why* and *how* human beings worked through the process of discovering alcohol takes us back to the earliest of human efforts at trial-and-error, yet the explanatory detail of what really occurred will probably always be left to our imaginations, couched by the reasoned inferences of scientists trying to reconstruct our past.

So, you ask, "What is this thing called 'fermentation'?" If you don't ask or if you're not interested, I'm going to tell you anyway.

We now know that as a routine part of nature's doings, invisible micro-organisms called *yeast*, which float in the air, routinely settle on crushed fruit and digest the sugars in that fruit. That yeast breaks down the atoms of carbon, hydrogen, and oxygen in the sugar as a means of securing the food that it needs to survive and perpetuate itself. After being broken down by yeast, these atoms of carbon, hydrogen and oxygen recombine into ethyl alcohol and carbon dioxide. The term fermentation refers to that process; it refers to the intrusion of yeast into those atoms and their subsequent conversion into a food product for yeast.

The ethyl alcohol that emerges from this biodegradation process is actually a by-product – a "waste product" — of fermentation. As crude junior chemists are given to comment, ethyl alcohol is, for all intents and purposes, "yeast shit." As you might have guessed, however, alcohol manufactures and their retail sales personnel rarely employ that phrase in their advertising.

Whatever the nature of the first human use of alcohol, also known as *ethanol*, once it was discovered, alcohol was to eventually become a part of most human cultures, although in some cultures it is a rare and hidden use.

After their discovery of alcohol's use as a beverage, the members of some cultures have indeed frowned on its use and succeeded in greatly limiting its consumption. In fact, some religions regard even the most limited use of beverage alcohol to be sinful. To achieve this end, alcohol has been made illegal in some societies and theocracies, with varying degrees of severity for the punishment of violations. Muslims, Hindus and Buddhists completely ban beverage alcohol consumption, although the enforcement of such bans varies considerably in intensity and effectiveness between countries in which these religions dominate.

It remains the case that alcohol consumption is a practice in almost all prehistoric, historic and contemporary cultures. In fact, even in those cultures that frown upon its use on religious grounds, the elite members and contrarians of those cultures privately indulge.

Mead

One of the first forms of beverage alcohol was a nutritious form of beer called *mead* or *honey wine*, as it is sometimes called, because it is made from fermented honey.

Mead was (and is today) a very thick beverage, much more densely viscous than beer, its contemporary descendant.

Historians have found records of mead-making that date back to approximately 1800 B.C., and they have observed that it was in common use around the year 8000 B.C.

Beer

Like its liquid ancestor, mead, which was widely savoured in its time, beer is an especially popular drink in the United States and Canada. In 2009, the American market for alcohol was $84.6 billion. Of that amount, beer represented by far the most common alcoholic beverage sold in the United States, with a market share of more than half of all sales of beverage alcohol. Spirits came second at $22.2 billion of the market, and wine came third, with $16.9 billion in sales. While roughly the same comparisons were evident in Canada a decade ago, in recent years beer has fallen to 46% (i.e., in 2010) of the market share of beverage alcohol sales, while wine has become increasingly popular, absorbing 29% of the retail market share. In 2010, spirits consumed about a quarter of the Canadian beverage alcohol sales. Thus, while the sales of spirits and wine differ between the two countries, in both, beer is well in the lead in the corporate race to sell recreational alcohol products.

The popularity of beer has much to do with the fact that individuals who identify with a wide variety of cultural and demographic sub-groups consider beer to be their drink of choice as their personal type drink, including truckers, cowboys, athletes, recreational skiers, youth, young adults, and, in terms of gender, men somewhat more than women. Taken together, all those membership groups in the beer drinking fraternity (and smaller sorority) add up to a solid majority. Beer has also long had the reputation of being a "working man's drink," in contrast to wines and "hard" liquor. This reputation was probably gained several decades ago when the retail price for the same volume of actual content in beer was much lower than other forms of drink. It is my impression, however, that, in recent years, the price of beer has escalated substantially in most jurisdictions. This is certainly the case in Canada and this trend may be responsible for the growing market share that wine is corralling north of the border.

Beer is made from malted barley, hops, maize and sugar. The barley is cleaned, sized and malted, the latter involving a process that soaks water into the barley when it is placed in deep tanks. The barley stays in those tanks until it has the proper moisture content for sprouting. This moistened barley is next placed in huge compartments to germinate. In those compartments, air is gently blown through it. When sprouting begins, the beer is then placed in kilns where heat is employed to stop the growth. The amount of heat and length of time the beer is in the kiln determines the colour of the final beer product.

After malting, both the ground barley malt and maize are mixed in proportion and then saturated with water in mashing tanks. During mashing, the starches are exposed to specific temperatures that turn the starches in the malt into fermentable sugars. Subsequently, the grains are strained off, which leaves a clear amber liquid called "wort." To this liquid, hops are added.

Richard W. Thatcher

Hops are the female flower clusters in a specific plant referred to as *Humulus Lupulus*. These flowers are commonly called seed cones or strobiles and are used primarily as a flavoring and stability agent in beer, giving it a tangy, slightly bitter taste.

In the making of beer, the mixed blend of wort and hops are brewed and subsequently cooled. Yeast is then added, as in mead, which ferments the sugars into alcohol and carbon dioxide. After a few subsequent days, the brewed product is placed in additional fermentation tanks where, with the help of controlled temperature, it sits until it has reached an acceptable level of alcohol and sugar. The yeast is then drained off and the beer sits for a few weeks until it builds up carbonation and flavour. Once the beer reaches what brew masters consider maturity, it flows through a final filter into filling machines. At this point, the beer is now ready for bottling and distribution.

Wine

Records of wine use are a little more recent than the documentation of human beer consumption but they still indicate a very lengthy history of this incarnation of beverage alcohol. According to some historians, wines made from the juice of berries have been dated as far back as (approximately) 6400 B.C. Wines from grapes have been dated to approximately 3500 B.C.

Many cultures utilize wine as a mainstay of their basic food and beverage supply, viewing it less as an alcoholic beverage than as an appetizing, nutritious part of their diet and as a flavourful and nutritious drink that is used to accompany ordinary meals. In other words, wine is often used in food preparation and as an enjoyable part of meals. Because of its alcohol content, wine is often employed for its preservative function in the preparation of some foods, and it can lend exquisitely delicious flavouring to a wide variety of foods.

In earlier periods of human history, in many cultures that no longer exist, as well as in many parts of the world today, wine is a far safer beverage than a cup of liquid from your locally available water supply. Its alcoholic contents are a great germ killer and its very production is, in part, a purification process.

Spirits ('Hard' Liquor)

As you will know, the other common beverage alcohol in widespread use is "hard liquor," which is sometimes called "spirits."

Historians seem to be in general agreement that the distilling of vegetables and grains for the purposes of producing spirits originated in Greco-Roman cultures around the year A.D. 800.

Apparently, through contact with the Greeks and Romans of antiquity, some Arabian tribes learned the distilling process. In turn, the Arabs are believed to have passed on the process for making hard liquor to other European cultures on the more northern reaches of the continent. Through trade contact with adventurous, early European commercial mariners, Asian countries also acquired a taste for alcohol, producing some of their own, distinctive drinks, such as Saki, the version so popular among the Japanese.

It was the distillation process that rendered imperishable food crops that would otherwise have rotted (biodegraded) too soon in storage or during transport to distant trading partners. As an alcoholic beverage, distilled spirits, like whiskey or rum, were cheaper and easier to ship than wine or beer. As international contacts and trade expanded over time, distilled spirits gradually became a favoured type of beverage alcohol in various parts of the globe.

Early refrigeration techniques were essentially cold rooms and underground containers. These techniques could only sustain the food use of a potato or other vegetables for a single period lying between their growing seasons. By distilling the "essence" or "spirits" of a food product, it could be maintained indefinitely.

Distillation is a process that is needed to push alcohol concentration above the 15% limit set by natural fermentation. In the distillation process, the wine obtained from fermentation is heated, causing some of the alcohol content to boil off as a vapour, or steam.

Alcohol boils at a much lower temperature than water, so its steam contains more alcohol than water vapour. When the steam from the wine is allowed to cool down, it reforms as a liquid with a higher concentration of alcohol and a lower concentration of water than the original wine from which it came. The vapour is collected in a cooling coil, out of which it drips into a container, like the copper kettle in the famous song of the same name. The combination of coil and collection vessel amalgamated in one contraption called a "still," a slang, root word derived from the word distillation itself.

The Benefits of Beverage Alcohol: They are Real and They are Many

Even if one is adamantly opposed to any kind of beverage alcohol use, the evidence does force any reasonable person to acknowledge that the practice has had and continues to have some significant benefits for humankind. I've mentioned a few such advantages already but, in fact, the drinking of alcoholic beverages offers many. We've been at it a long, long time, and there is little sign that this indulgence will abate significantly in the near, medium or distant future. The truth is that beverage alcohol consumption is tightly knitted into the very fabric of most societies, perhaps nowhere more so than North America.

If beverage alcohol had no valuable use and no fundamental and common appeal, surely it wouldn't be so widely used and so commonly accepted. After all, it is one of the very few widely legalized recreational, mood-modifying drugs, albeit with many restrictions accompanying its manufacture, sale and use. Coffee and tobacco share the same space but their capacity for mood-modification is very minor compared with alcohol, street drugs or various inappropriately used, medically prescribed pharmaceuticals.

I've noted some of the benefits of beverage alcohol above, including its usefulness as a germ free liquid sometimes needed when water quality is substandard and in the preservation of the essence of vegetables. But there are many more. Below I've compiled a list of some of the uses and distinctive benefits of beverage alcohol in human societies.

1. The Role of Alcohol in Religious Rites

In some instances, alcohol is invested with a sacred significance. Consider the fact that, in societies in which Christianity prevails, wine is treated as being representative of the free-flowing blood of Christ. Sipping wine is a central part of the religious rituals of communion in the Anglican, Episcopalian and Roman Catholic churches.

Beverage alcohol has been described as the elusive elixir of eternal life by the ancient alchemists who tried to isolate its soul and spirit (and, in the process, they probably gave the name 'spirits' to their earliest, rudimental distillates) in order to secure the offerings of a bountiful nature spilling forth its annual crops of berries containing fermentable juices. It has thus been used in religious rituals in not only Christian communion but in the religious rituals of many cultures.

While the concrete benefit and necessity of alcohol in religious practice is obviously debatable, if not downright questionable, there is a case for some very real benefits of beverage alcohol. Let me list some of the better known of such benefits.

2. Physical Health Benefits

There are a variety of physical benefits offered up by beverage alcohol. Consider the following:

- **Alcohol as a Pain-killer**

Beverage alcohol has long been used for its medicinal value, especially as a pain reliever for those undergoing primitive forms of surgery or anticipating or actually experiencing unbearable pain. The most obvious example is the provision of alcohol to injured victims during rescue efforts.

You might have seen pictures of those small wooden drums of alcohol hanging from the collars of Saint Bernard dogs on Swiss mountain rescue teams. Alcohol actually does act pretty effectively on the nerve signals to numb the hurt physical pain.

In early western movies and television series like *Gunsmoke*, there was often a kindly doctor, situated on the second floor of a building on or just off main street, who offered an injured cowboy or a felled gunfighter a few strong swigs of alcohol before extracting a bullet or performing surgery in a life and death situation. That scenario wasn't just the fantasy of Hollywood imaginations. Alcohol, taken at intoxicating levels, was long used in the medical treatment prior to the incorporation of other forms of anaesthetics in the performance of surgery. It was commonplace in the military as an antidote to pain. Alcohol is a blessing in such circumstances because alcoholic intoxication numbs one's reactions to physical trauma. In fact, when sophisticated medical care is not available, it is still used.

You've probably all heard about people with very troubled backgrounds "self-medicating" with alcohol to relieve or purge their emotional pain from their immediate consciousness. Depending on the circumstances, the approach is not recommended. However, until you or I walk in the shoes of experience of any specific individual who uses alcohol for these purposes, it's probably not appropriate to dismiss the value of the remedy out of hand. Alcohol does function effectively to relieve anxiety for many people.

- **Alcohol as Part of Healthy Human Diets**

Alcohol, especially wine and beer but also spirits, have long been used as part of cooking, lending not only flavour and some substance to the food but also some protection against the toxicity created by the aging or undercooking of food. As I noted above, *mead*, a form of beer made from fermented honey, was in common use 10,000 years ago. This thick liquid had considerable food value, providing necessary vitamins and amino acids to the diet of the drinker. By comparison, modern beers are not nearly as nutritious, but they are also invested with very real food value.

- **Alcohol as a *Preventive* Medicine**

Overall Physical Health. Moderate drinking does seem to be associated with overall physical health. Don't get me wrong, it is possible that moderate drinking is associated with moderate living, while *both* total abstinence and heavy drinking are associated with a generally less healthy psychological state. It remains the case that moderate drinking has been consistently associated with various dimensions of elevated physical health in a variety of scientific studies.

Decreased Heart Attack Risks and General Enhancement of Heart Health. As early as the turn of the 19th into the 20th century, research evidence indicated that moderate alcohol consumption was associated with a decreased risk for heart attacks. In fact, reviews of scientific research evidence have been pretty consistent in reporting a strong relationship between moderate alcohol consumption and reduction in heart attacks, cardiovascular disease and coronary artery disease in particular. The National Institute of Alcohol Abuse and Alcoholism (NIAAA) acknowledges the validity of research indicating that moderate drinking is beneficial to heart health. In fact, moderate drinking, as a behaviour, is associated with a sharp decrease in the risk of heart disease (from 40% to 60% is reported in various scientific studies). British and Chinese studies have provided similar evidence. These findings are most significant because cardiovascular (heart) disease is the number one cause of death in the United States and Canada. It is now believed that 1-2 drinks per day, primarily of red wine, is associated with a 25% reduction in the risk of heart attacks among males.

Prevention of a variety of diseases. The research suggests that sensible drinking also appears to be beneficial for physical health by reducing or preventing various other common diseases. These include diabetes, rheumatoid arthritis, osteoporosis and bone fractures, kidney stones, digestive ailments, stress and depression, poor cognition and memory, Parkinson's disease, hepatitis A, pancreatic cancer, macular degeneration (which is a major cause of blindness in senior years), angina pectoris, ulcers, erectile dysfunction, hearing loss, gallstones, liver disease and poor physical condition in the elderly. The statistical evidence now indicates that the tendency for a greater length of life for moderate drinkers is associated with a reduction of such diseases as coronary heart disease, cancer, and respiratory diseases.

Decreased Cancer Risks. Sound research suggests that a compound found only in hops and the main product they're used in, namely beer, is effective in preventing many types of cancer. The darker the brew, the higher the concentration of this active ingredient. This flavanoid compound called *Xanthohumol* is lethal to prostate, breast, colon, and ovarian cancer cells. Thus, moderate beer consumption seems to lower the risk of some cancers.

Studies show that, at least in rats, this compound stops tumour growth at an early age.

> **WARNING: Some researchers believe that the various physical health benefits of moderate drinking may have been inflated.** While the balance of evidence does support the idea that regular but very limited amounts of alcohol, especially red wine, can produce various health benefits, as with any scientific conclusion, some research challenges this view—and, in the future, new evidence might undermine current thinking.
>
> But don't forget that it is *moderate* drinking that is associated with specific health benefits; it is *not* heavy drinking.

Increased Life Expectancy. An extensive review of research by the National Institute of Alcohol Abuse and Alcoholism (NIAAA) has reported that light and moderate drinkers have the greatest chance of living a long life.

Preventing and "Slowing" Alzheimer's Disease. There is recent evidence that moderate drinking may prevent or stave off Alzheimer's disease. Alzheimer's is the leading cause of *dementia*, which involves deterioration in one's thinking capacity. That deterioration includes the wandering of one's attention, a reduction of awareness of one's surroundings and immediate social circumstances, and immediate, anticipated word recovery often fails and memory in general is impaired. In Alzheimer's disease, specific parts of the brain degenerate, destroying cells and reducing the responsiveness of the remaining ones to many of the chemicals that transmit signals to the brain. As indicated in autopsies of Alzheimer patients, abnormal tissues, referred to by physicians as "senile plaques" and abnormal proteins appear in the brain when this condition takes hold. In a study reported in the February, 2009 issue of the journal, *Alcoholism: Clinical and Experimental Research*, University of Chicago researchers provided evidence that people who have one to two alcoholic drinks a day are often at lower risk of developing Alzheimer's disease and dementia than their teetotalling peers (See Collins *et al*, 2009). The investigators analysed the findings of 44 studies of moderate alcohol intake and its effects on the heart and brain. The researchers, supported by detailed reviews by seven American scientists, have concluded that alcohol appears to trigger a protective state by occupying the same biochemical pathways which, left open, result in heart problems, Alzheimer's and dementia (impairment of thinking capacity).

Preventing Weight Gain. A recent study has suggested that moderate drinking by women over thirty may actually function as a weight loss drug. Recent research at Boston's Brigham and Women's Hospital published in the *Archives of Internal Medicine* examined data on 19,000 women aged 39 and older who were not overweight when the study began. They found that the women in the study who drank from 15 to less than 30 grams of alcohol a day were 30% less likely than the teetotallers (non-drinkers) studied to become overweight or obese during the time the study was undertaken. A typical, non-light beer, 8 ounce glass of wine, or single-shot cocktail contains about 15 grams of alcohol. Over an average of 13 years of follow-up, most of the women in the study gained some weight but the teetotaller gained the most and those who reported drinking no more than two drinks a day gained the least. The researchers claim that they do not know what the mechanism causing the differences in weight gain is, including whether it is psychological or biological, however. Nor do they advise women to drink as a means of achieving weight control or weight loss. In fact, they caution that it would not be a good idea for women who do not drink to take it up in order to keep from gaining weight.

3. Alcohol as Handmaiden to Relaxation and Psychic Freedom

In addition to these specific health and nutritional benefits, beverage alcohol provides a variety of pleasures, satisfactions and useful functions for human beings, including its power to relax and relieve anxiety. While currently being challenged[2], many scientists have suggested that this relief

---

2   More recent interpretations of the effects of alcohol are referred to as the "Myopia effect," which suggests that the real effect of alcohol impairment is to simplify the drinker's cognition by obscuring the detail of peripheral visual and cognitive considerations and enhancing the drinker's focus on whatever is in his immediate field of vision or thinking. The result is not necessarily a loss of inhibition, but an uncluttered focus on the present and foreground. While background factors

and relaxation effect is due to what is referred to as a "disinhibition effect," which, in lay terms, means that when we have several drinks, our feeling that we must repress our extreme feelings subsides. In short, we lose our inhibitions as our drinking proceeds. This lowering of inhibitions has long been considered an excellent aid to celebrations, a source of tension relief when taken in small doses, and a comfort while mourning the passing of a loved one. The relaxation that comes with a drink or two makes light conversation and mingling easier and, arguably, it socially lubricates the path to sexual intimacies, especially when taken by two parties.

4. Positive Social Functions

There is evidence that drinking has various other positive social functions as well.

- **Beverage Alcohol as an Aid to Social Bonding**

Studies dating back several decades that have focussed on Native American and Canadian First Nations and Inuit found positive as well as negative aspects to the drinking behaviour of Native North Americans. Anthropologist Dwight Heath's study of the Navajo suggested that social bonding within their own communities was enhanced by drinking together, often in ritualized ceremonies (1964).

Students of Aboriginal cultures, the anthropologists Craig MacAndrew and Robert B. Edgerton (1969) observed that social drinking among the Tarahumara of northern Mexico was a crucial element of and support for their religion, economy, entertainment, dispute settlement, and marriage arrangements.

- **Alcohol as an Aid to Overcoming Shyness and Expressed Hidden Feelings**

Anthropologist Jack Ferguson (1971) suggested that when drinking was introduced to the Aboriginal peoples in the Arctic by White whalers,

---

recede, the foreground is enhanced and that foreground may be a very happy and distracting one or a set of anger-inducing or depression-inducing thoughts that trigger sluggish passivity or acting out in anger or even rage.

it became a substitute for traditional shamanism. He was referring to traditional supernatural beliefs guided by individual shaman who presumably had special powers of insight, healing and connection with "spirits." A shaman in pre-literate hunting and gathering societies, as well as early horticultural, fishing and initial agrarian cultures, were regarded as spiritual, ceremonial and herbal advisors and healers.

The same anthropologist suggested that drinking for the Inuit (formerly referred to as Eskimos) also became an outlet for individualistic behaviour in cultures in which any deviation from norms or traditions was frowned upon and typically repressed. Other scholars have made similar observations.

Ronald and Evelyn Rohner (1970), also anthropologists, have argued that, at least until recently, drinking had a positive function among the Kwakiutl of British Columbia. The Rohners' research convinced them that the drinking experience can relax communications that are normally very restrictive. Thus, drinking alcohol can encourage more open expression of affection and compliments as well as hostility. They found that even when hostile exchanges were the outcome, the fact that these emotions were expressed during a drinking session made for a ready excuse after the session was over, and a commonly accepted excuse that enabled a forgiving attitude. Similar observations have been made by other social scientists that have focussed on other ethnic and national populations, as well as modern societies.

- **Stimulating the Joy of Intense Humour**

Other writers have observed that drinking can be a handmaiden to mirth. Drinking sessions often provide an opportunity for the extremely enjoyable expression of humour—including humour that might not be acceptable in "dry" forums.

- **Beverage Alcohol Venues as Social Focal Points**

Specific gathering places centred on the serving of beverage alcohol have often served as social focal points for communities, like-minded people, or people with shared social circumstances. This is true for university students, as well as members of specialized occupations and business owners. Members of employee groups, professionals and social activists often congregate at specific "watering holes" where they find people with much in common, conduct some business, and get and share on updates on other matters of common interest.

It is also especially important for groups of the poor and disenfranchised. Public houses ("pubs"), saloons and bars have essentially served as social clubs, however unrefined, for Native Americans throughout North America. This is not restricted to Aboriginal people however. Rural and southern Whites migrating to towns and cities for employment, often have bars where they find old friends, acquaintances or simply peers from their own areas of origin. In these venues they find enjoyment, useful information and various forms of support while sharing in the liquid offerings of the establishment at which they are congregating. Latino, African-American and various recent immigrant and migrant groups also tend to concentrate in specific drinking establishments, populating them so completely that people outside their ethnic or social group tend to feel out of place when they make a visit. While these bars are frequently the site of serious and even tragic conflicts (some are the "tough" bars – some *very* tough), they are also welcoming drop-in centres, places where participants find their friends, strangers find people of similar background, and where individuals seek out and find intimates or find other people they are searching out. For people who feel alone and out of place far from their home, drinking spots are often the source of information exchanges about jobs, social services, even business opportunities.

The local neighbourhood drinking establishment, including bars close to or on college campuses, obviously does contribute positively to a sense of community amongst neighbours and between students. Such bars are places where many enjoyable things happen quite incidental to drinking alcohol, including socializing, playing darts, pool or video games, and securing a date.

- **Drinking as a Lubricant for Joyous Celebration**

While one may question the choice, many believe that drinking does accompany, enhance and relax the mood at various social functions. It is used as part of family and community gatherings and as part of calendar holidays and celebrations, such as Christmas. Even in excess use, it is very much a part of major community events and major cultural and sports functions from *Mardi Gras* to Super Bowl week to the Stanley Cup in hockey.

- **Ritualizing Times of Pleasurable Relief from the Stresses of Work and Learning**

Drinking also serves as a marker and relief-provider after surviving a gruelling week of work or after completing exams in high school, college or university. In all of these, along with the actual events themselves, the social experience offers a collective opportunity for an acceptable "time out," a circumstance in which excessive, otherwise unacceptable behaviour is actually given at least some measure of acceptance and forgiveness.

- **The Drinking Occasion as a Cement that Bonds Fellowship and Intimacy**

In fact, while drinking is associated with many negative outcomes, including various troubling social consequences, it can also be a social lubricant. At least for men, being a drinker may foster social networks that are very significant for life-long advances in one's personal fortunes. A study by the Reason Foundation found that both women and men, who are self-described drinkers, earn 10-14% more than non-drinkers. The same study also found that wages or salaries of men who visit bars at least once a month earn on average 7% more in wages than their colleagues who avoid bars. For women, bar-hopping had little effect. (See Peters and Stringham, 2006). The researchers contend that drinking may help build the kinds of social networks that lead to workplace success. While they didn't say it, it is also surely the case that frequent, heavy drinking and hostile, angry or just plain helpless, impaired behaviour when drinking can freeze problem drinkers out of the social networks that can advance their careers.

- **The Alcohol Industry Yields Significant Economic Benefits**

The alcoholic beverage industry is a job creator. It benefits individuals and the economy by employing many thousands of people in the manufacture, bottling, advertising and direct sales segments of the industry. In turn, it yields enormous gains for government in the form of taxes on alcoholic beverages and the various stages of production and distribution through which these beverages are processed and delivered and sold to consumers.

More on the False Wisdom of the 'Forbidden Fruit' Orientation to Alcohol in North America

Research has shown that cultures that accept responsible social drinking as a normal part of life tend to experience less alcohol abuse in their populations than cultures that fear and condemn its use.

Both medical and behavioural studies have shown that when a society adopts a perspective that fears and condemns alcohol, alcohol abuse becomes a much more widespread problem than those societies that treat it as a normal, even beneficial, but minor aspect of common lifestyles.

Based on the experience of other countries, several commentators have suggested that in creating a phalanx of restrictive rules and constantly sending out condemnatory public service messages about alcohol, North America has it all wrong. They suggest that the answer is to normalize alcohol use, teaching children from a young age how to use it. By employing positive role modeling and instructive socialization of children regarding alcohol use, parents themselves, if educated in the matter, can effectively teach responsible drinking to children and youth. These observers are supported by data from around the world showing that the adoption of a responsible drinking culture is far more effective than prohibitionist messages that condemn drinking and treat it as a "forbidden fruit."

In North America, several ethnic groups have tended to import cultural norms about drinking to North America and this has shielded their children from the excessive alcohol abuse on this continent. Italian, Jewish and Chinese Americans learned to drink moderately as they were growing up. Raised in homes in which an alcoholic beverage was deemed an ordinary part of life, they were taught that excess drinking was inappropriate and rude. This approach is reflected in the homes of several transplanted generations. Italian-, Jewish- and Chinese-Americans grow up drinking moderately in homes in which the practice is viewed as a normal part of life, while heavy drinking is condemned. By contrast, those from northern European countries, which, with the exception of France, tend to strongly condemn alcohol use and alcohol abuse is a major problem.

A Concluding Comment on the Positive Side of Drinking

I am not advocating the use of alcohol as the only solution to the various psychological, social or medical needs it has and continues to meet for many millions of human beings around the world. In fact, in most cases, there are, at least potentially, better – and usually far better — alternatives to the human functions that alcoholic beverages are exploited to serve. Many alternatives have proven to be far more advantageous and far less likely to lead to negative consequences.

In short, drinking alcoholic beverages is a pretty human thing to do, and it has more than a few things to offer us. Like anger, sex, caution, bravery, or salty or sugary foods, however, alcohol is only beneficial if we employ it in a reasonable way. The big question is *what* is reasonable?

Chapter 4

Volume of Alcohol Consumed and Drunkenness

So what is a reasonable amount of alcohol consumption during any drinking session?

In most instances, you should exclude actual intoxication from your list of reasonable and personally and socially acceptable behaviours. As a rule, getting drunk is ill-advised.

I also want to address those exceptions, however. I recognize that, on some occasions, having a few extra drinks is extremely tempting. Under circumstances in which safety can virtually be assured, drinking heavily to celebrate a significant, transitional event in your life or the life of a friend may be hard to avoid. Admittedly, it can also be a lot of fun. A most significant question then is, by degree, how much will it take to significantly impair your judgement?

When you feel that you have lost a little control, make no mistake, you are venturing into a high risk situation—and the more you drink, the riskier the situation. Measuring your blood alcohol level is usually a pretty fair measure of what it takes to get you drunk—and I encourage you to figure that out in controlled circumstances.

You should also be aware that both the extent of your intoxication and the risks attending the drinking episode *can* be tempered by engineering the situation in advance to maximize safety. I repeat: I am clearly not encouraging you to get drunk but I do recognize that it might occasionally happen. So in your own defence and in the defence of others, I encourage you to adopt strategies that will minimize the harm that might occur during that binge.

Intoxication levels are largely pumped up by how much you drink, which is to say, by the amount of alcohol in your blood. Usually referred to as your 'BAC' (i.e., you "blood alcohol concentration"), this level can be estimated with reasonable accuracy. This accuracy is possible because, although the absorption of alcohol by the human body is quite variable, metabolism itself occurs at a defined, continuous rate.

About one ounce of pure alcohol is eliminated from the body every 3 hours. We can therefore usually predict the actual amount of alcohol that will be circulating through the body and brain and how long that amount will take to be metabolized by the liver and excreted through urination, breathing and sweating.

It takes about 15-20 minutes for alcohol to reach the brain by way of the blood, thus beginning the impairment process, but more time for it to enter the urine. According to the NIAAA (1997), it takes 30-40 minutes after ingestion to reach maximum blood alcohol concentration.

The BAC table provided in the appendix shows measures of the concentration of alcohol in a drinker's blood. While a person's actual reaction and level of impairment in response to these measured concentrations can vary, depending on drinking history, psychological tolerance, and several other factors, these BAC measures do provide a fairly accurate indication of the concentration of alcohol in the blood and the associated level of impairment. In fact, such measures are used by the courts to determine whether a driver's blood alcohol level is above a legally established limit that is treated as the threshold for being charged driving while impaired (DUI).

The unit of measure for BAC is weight by volume, for example, milligrams per decilitre, although it can be expressed as a percentage. The BAC is usually recorded in milligrams of alcohol per 100 millilitres of blood) or milligrams per centum, which, abbreviated, reads "mg%"). However, the BAC is usually expressed simply as a decimal, such as the most commonly known threshold of legal ".08," expressed without the % sign altogether (By the way, in most jurisdictions, that .08 has been reduced significantly or such a reduction is being seriously considered). This figure is just mg%

divided by 1,000, which means moving the decimal point three digits to the left.

Highway patrols and urban police can provide a reasonably accurate estimate of one's BAC with the aid of a breath sample, taken with a measurement instrument known as a breathalyser that you blow into. This is commonly known as a breathalyser test.

If a 200 lb. man has 5 drinks in 2 hours, his blood alcohol would be .108 minus the timetable factor of .030, leaving his BAC at .078, and he would be legally able to drive in most states because ".08" has long been the accepted standard (although many want the rate to be lowered to .05). By the same token, if his wife, who was 150 lbs. also had 5 drinks over 2 hours that evening, her blood alcohol concentration would be .169 minus the timetable factor of .030. At .130, her BAC would be too high for her to drive.

We'll get into specific drinking self-management strategies in detail later and, in that wider context, I will again discuss blood alcohol levels and drinking limits.

You shouldn't underestimate the power of alcohol. Alcohol acts fast and it doesn't take long for it to impair your capacity to think and act. Drawing upon the University of Oklahoma's *Police Notebook* website and a book by William R. Miller and Ricardo F. Munoz entitled *Controlling Your Drinking* (2005), the following summary provides a pretty good idea of the psychological and physical reactions by the light and moderate drinker to blood alcohol (BAC) levels at intensifying elevations (*Note*: I am referring to light and moderate drinkers to the exclusion of frequent, heavy drinkers and chronic alcohol-dependents who have much higher tolerance levels):

- Light and moderate drinkers begin to feel very modest effects when their BAC level reaches .02, which is the approximate level reached after one drink. When BAC is between .02 and .03, there is no loss of coordination. There is also a slight euphoria (elevated, positive feelings), and a loss of shyness and most people get slightly depressed after the feeling of euphoria, mildly relaxed and a little light headed.

Thinkin' Drinkin'

- Around .04, most light and moderate drinkers begin to feel a little relaxed. There is a feeling of well-being and relaxation, lowered inhibitions, and a sensation of warmth. At this level there is enough impairment in reaction time and fine motor skills that driving is slightly affected. Some countries have made it illegal to drive at this level. There is also minor impairment of reasoning and memory, and a lowering of a protective sense of caution. Sometimes one's behaviour becomes exaggerated and emotions are intensified (which means that negative emotions are heightened and positive emotions are increased).

- At .55, any positive effects of beverage alcohol will have been realized and the effects morph into being almost completely negative. Perception, judgement, memory, learning, coordination, sexual arousal, alertness, and self-control all begin to deteriorate.

- At .06, judgement is impaired. People are less able to make rational decisions about their capabilities to handle complex tasks, to swim, play a sport, fight, to ride a bike, motorcycle or drive a car or other vehicle, such as a motorboat, or snowmobile.

- Between .07 and .09, there is slight impairment of balance, speech, vision, hearing and reaction time. Judgement and self-control tends to be reduced and reasoning, memory and caution are impaired. Of great significance, at .08% muscle coordination and driving skills are impaired for light and moderate drinkers. This remains the legal intoxication limit for driving in most states but that figure is being lowered, as it has already been in most Canadian provinces.

- At .10 BAC to .125 BAC, there is, typically, significant impairment of motor coordination and loss of good judgement. Speech is often slurred and balance, vision, reaction time and hearing are impaired. There is clear deterioration in memory, reaction time, and the control and coordination of movements. At .12, vomiting usually occurs, unless this level is reached very slowly or a person has developed a tolerance for alcohol. Vomiting is the body's first line defence against overdose, according to Miller and Munoz and other substance abuse researchers.

- At .15 the balance of a light or moderate drinker is impaired and walking in a straight line is a significant challenge, typically not achieved. The BAC level in the bloodstream is equivalent to one-half pint of whiskey circulating in the bloodstream. There is gross impairment of motor skills and a lack of physical control. The blurring of vision intensifies and balance is even more of a challenge. The feeling of euphoria diminishes, replaced by depressive effects. Judgement and perception in general are severely impaired.

- At .16 to .19, feelings of depression predominate and the drinker may experience nausea. At this level, diminished reasoning, judgement and motor (muscular) control is characteristic.

- At around .20, it is common to feel dazed and confused. The individual may need help to walk. Physical pain is substantially diminished. The gag reflex is impaired at this level so one can choke if vomiting occurs. Many people experience a blackout at this level, which means that, the following day, they will have significant patches of memory loss regarding the events that took place during their drinking episode.

- As the BAC level increases beyond .20, all mental, physical and sensory functions are acutely impaired. If the individual vomits, there is an increased risk of asphyxiation. There is also a considerable risk of serious injury as a result of falls and other accidents. At .30%, most people will lose consciousness. Scientists regard this loss of consciousness as the last of the body's natural defences against the risks of the bender.

- At .30, BAC and individual's thinking can best be described as "stupor." In other words, one has little comprehension of where one is and passing out is very likely.

- At .35, going into a coma is very possible.

- The individual adult with an average tolerance for alcohol is likely to die from alcohol poisoning once the BAC level reaches .45. At this level, the breathing and heartbeat of the normally light and moderate drinker will probably stop.

As noted, these percentages will vary with tolerance, which grows with frequent repetition over time, as well as with sex and weight and length of the drinking episode.[3] Because I am primarily addressing the impact of alcohol on the inebriation of youth, few of whom are chronic alcoholics with high tolerance levels, I have included in the appendix charts that indicate BAC levels per drink by sex and weight and time of the drinking episode.

Table 1

Number of Drinks and BAC Level After One Hour of Drinking

5 drinks	.10	
	.09	
	.08	3 drinks
4 drinks	.07	
	.06	
3 drinks	.05	2 drinks
	.04	
2 drinks	.03	
	.02	
	.01	
170 lb. Male	BAC	137 lb. Female

The chart above indicates the average increase in BAC per drink for light and moderate male and female drinkers who have been drinking over one hour. The subsequent chart indicates the same comparison over two hours.

---

3 **Note:** The effects of alcohol intoxication are greatly influenced by individual variations. Thus, it may take more or less of these consumption levels to produce the same effects.

Table 2

Number of Drinks and BAC Level in Two Hours of Drinking

	.10	4 drinks
	.09	
5 drinks	.08	
	.07	3 drinks
4 drinks	.06	
	.05	
	.04	
3 drinks	.03	2 drinks
	.02	
2 drinks	.01	
170 lb. Male		137 lb. Female

Chapter 5

The Stinkin' Consequences of Careless Drinking

As I have explained above, at least when undertaken in moderation, beverage alcohol has provided – and continues to provide – some very real benefits for humankind. With justification, its many functions in various cultures can be celebrated. Yet when drinking results in intoxication and is motivated by troubled attitudes, psychological stress or anti-social thoughts and feelings, it often results in an overwhelming dose of emotional pain, physical injury, fatalities and, of course, permanent and profound regrets by drinkers and, so very often, their victims.

Alcohol Problems in the Media: So Common they aren't 'Newsworthy'

It is worth considering the irony in the gap between the limited public concern about alcohol problems and the attention paid to other mood-modifying substances. Like drugs that profoundly affect your thinking and emotional state, alcohol is used for several reasons, including purely recreational purposes, for self-medication to relieve emotional pain, and, sometimes, merely as an aid to temporary relief from the boredom of routine or the episodic tensions of daily life.

While beverage alcohol is the most widespread chemical substance chosen by human beings for significant mood-modification, it is also the most widely legalized and readily available of all such substances in widespread use. Despite a far greater overall toll in human costs than other drugs, far less attention is paid to it than a number of other drugs that exact far fewer overall costs to individuals, communities and societies as a whole.

Consider the enormous public attention paid in the past few years to "Crystal Meth" (a recently popularized form of methamphetamine), and the "War on Drugs" waged by the U.S. Government against heroin, cocaine (including 'crack'), and even the relatively benign marijuana; then compare that to the relative quietude surrounding alcohol abuse.

> Alcohol is so much an accepted part of our life that it is hard to draw serious public policy attention to its darker side. Other than when it is occasionally sensationalized, problem drinking, as news, is considered a bit of a yawn and the limited coverage of the issue by the media reflects this disinterest.

There is a sense in which alcohol problems have become mundane as an item of topical conversation or of public interest.

Like beverage alcohol itself, personal and interpersonal problems in which alcohol consumption is in some way implicated are so ever-present, so routine, so expected, that we simply accept them without much thought. They are commonplace, like the weather, the darkness of night and lightness of day, and the changing of the seasons. Alcohol problems are ever and everywhere with us, if not in the immediate present then it is always close at hand; if not in our own homes, then in the homes of uncles, aunts and cousins, or the households of friends and neighbours.

It is more than a little noteworthy that, unlike many other mood-altering drugs, alcoholic beverages can be legally and readily purchased at the local shopping centre, in many American jurisdictions on corner stores on every other block (at least in densely populated urban neighbourhoods), and in specialized liquor outlets in small cities and towns throughout the United States and Canada. Beverage alcohol is on hand at most parties, celebratory events, and it is part of the regular fare of local bars and taverns, as well as an accompaniment to meals in restaurants of all kinds.

It is also available in the food and beverage sections of urban airports of substantial size and for sale at most major sporting events.

In terms of newsworthiness and the public appetite for new stories (i.e., 'news'), there is something seemingly exotic about "street drugs," at least outside extremely impoverished or crime-blighted areas of large cities where they have become commonplace. Alcohol, on the other hand, is on hand in most households. It is pervasive in the normal course of contemporary life and it has been for centuries. As a result, as a topic of everyday discourse, alcohol, even in terms of the problems it creates, is viewed as, well, a bit of a yawn, and thus, as a public health concern, it simply doesn't get the focussed attention it warrants.

Let me provide you with a summary of some of the most common and most injurious results of careless drinking.

Beverage Alcohol Ingestion and its Effects on the Human Body

The molecules that make up ethanol are easily and quickly absorbed into the human body. After a drink is swallowed it enters the stomach and small intestine. In those tracts, a large number of blood vessels make a person's blood readily accessible to swallowed alcohol. Approximately 20 percent of any dose of alcohol is absorbed through the stomach, with the balance of the dose being absorbed through the small intestine.

After alcohol enters the bloodstream, its molecules are circulated throughout the body, coming into direct contact with the cells of all the body's organs.

As a drug, alcohol *is* a Central Nervous System (CNS) *Depressant*, despite the fact that, typically, it initially creates a stimulating effect. That initial effect has led to the common assumption that alcohol is a stimulant. The reason for this confusion is that, at low doses, alcohol first impairs the capacity of the part of the brain called the "cerebral cortex" to perform one of its normal tasks, which is to inhibit the urges created by the subcortical parts of the brain. In other words, alcohol depresses an area of the brain that normally would be an inhibitor, and the result is an illusion of stimulation. As the drinking bout proceeds, however, a sense of sadness and a darkening of thinking processes emerge.

Tolerance, Blood Alcohol Concentration and Weight Differences

One of the most significant factors that can affect your response to alcohol is *tolerance*. In the context of beverage alcohol consumption, tolerance results from the body's attempt to stay in balance despite regular alcohol consumption. Some scientific research suggests that there are variations in our tolerance, based on a number of factors, including your inherited bio-chemistry or, in other words, your genetics.

When you develop increased tolerance by drinking increasing amounts of alcohol over time, you experience a reduction in the intensity of that initial, stimulating effect you received from a drink. Many take this as a positive sign that they can now hold their liquor better and stay more in control. But in fact, that very tolerance reduces one's ability to feel pleasure from small amounts of alcohol and it also seems to increase the depressing effects of higher doses.

As tolerance develops, the "had enough" signal that your body sends to your brain to tell you to stop drinking (which non-problem drinkers recognize and respond to) is diminished or lost. People with greater levels of tolerance are likely to drink more as a result. And so tolerance leads to increased consumption and thus exposes your body to higher blood alcohol concentration and, as a result, a greater probability of negative health consequences.

As indicated in the previous chapter, one way to understand and control the effects of alcohol is to know about and use information regarding your blood alcohol concentration (shortened to 'BAC,' for convenience). Your BAC is directly related to how much you drink: the more alcohol you consume; the higher your BAC.

The BAC that results from a given amount of alcohol also varies by weight, the time-span in which the alcohol is consumed, and whether or not you are a male or female. It's easy to see why most of these factors matter. The more you weigh, the more fluid you will have in your body, so any given dose of alcohol will be more diluted and less impairing. The more time that has passed since you consumed alcohol, the more time your body will have had to metabolize it and get it out of your system.

Sex Differences

The difference in the impact of alcohol on males and females is a bit more complicated. For a number of reasons, women tend to achieve higher BACs from the same amount of alcohol consumed by men. Women, of course, weigh less on average, but they also have a higher proportion of fat in their bodies in relation to water, so, compared to men, they have relatively less water to dilute the alcohol. In addition, women have less of the gastric enzyme that metabolizes and deactivates alcohol.

A 120-pound woman would have a .027 BAC an hour after drinking one drink, a 0071 BAC after two drinks in one hour, and would be just at the 0.055% BAC after two drinks in two hours. But if a 180-pound man consumes two drinks in two hours, his BAC will be only 0.016 percent. The differences by sex and weight, as you can see, can be quite dramatic. Some other relevant facts about the distinctive impact of drinking on females include the following:

- As a result of differences in the capacity of male and female stomachs to oxidize alcohol and the production of less alcohol dehydrogenase, the enzyme that breaks alcohol down, women tend to have more alcohol enter their bloodstream.

- Adolescent females (and women) tend to get intoxicated more quickly just before menstruation (their period) than they do at other times.

- The weight of evidence indicates that females tend to develop alcohol dependency more rapidly than men.

- Women taking birth control pills tend to have higher blood pressure levels when they drink. This is because the liver metabolizes *both* the pills and the alcohol at the same time.

- Some studies suggest that, more often than, compared with men, women are more likely to begin drinking alcohol heavily because of a specific, negative circumstance or stressor, which they may use to self-medicate.

- Female alcohol abuse is often associated with a biography that includes sexual abuse. In fact, females are more likely than men to have experienced sexually-related trauma resulting in sexual dysfunction and many use alcohol to gain comfort in engaging in sexual activities.

- There is some evidence that women may be more susceptible to cognitive problems – reduction in clear and rational thinking – related to drinking.

Negative Health Outcomes: Physical Health and Safety Risks

Let's consider the entire range of excessive drinking and the problems associated with it.

I've already noted the matter of over-drinking styles being a gateway to addictive alcohol and drug abuse. Let me review some other facts.

Too much drinking poses high risks to the health of anyone who indulges in beverage alcohol, whether or not they are a habitual drinking physically or psychologically dependent on the drug. For example:

- Alcohol consumption also poses risks for diabetics because the disorder makes it difficult for the human body to process the high sugar contents in most alcohol.

- Too much drinking also alters and kills brain cells; impairs memory, coordination, and judgement. Heavy drinking may damage the connection between nerve cells and cause brain damage, which is irreversible.

- When persisting over the long term, excessive consumption of alcohol increases the risk of heart disease and stroke. It causes high blood pressure, although this is mostly a problem of alcoholics, some of whom suffer from deterioration of the heart muscle and other forms of heart disease. Regular, heavy drinking also elevates the risk of anaemia.

- Over-drinking on a regular or frequent but occasional basis also irritates the gastrointestinal system, blocking absorption of essential nutrients. This can cause gastritis and ulcers.

- Regular over-drinking also increases the risk of some cancers, and can cause cirrhosis of the liver.

- Regular over-drinking also leaches calcium from the bones, which can make an existing condition of osteoporosis deteriorate.

- Heavy alcohol use by men reduces the level of testosterone and can stimulate the growth of feminine-like physical features – breast development and shrinkage of the testicles – and produce impotence.

- Heavy drinking among women, even a few episodes, can result in fetal alcohol spectrum disorder in their offspring. FASD is a tragically common condition associated with low birth weight, varying degrees of intellectual impairment, limited capacity for autonomous moral judgement and, in severe cases, mild deformity of the facial and eye structure. Every year, the consequences of FASD cost society billions of dollars in terms of specially supported services. African-American and Native American (and First Nations) women are at particular risk of passing FASD on to their offspring. African American women are 7 times as likely to pass it on as American women generally, and Native American women more than 4 times as likely (*Note*: There is more on FASD below).

- Women who over-drink regularly do so at increased risk of experiencing menstrual difficulties.

- Women who drink are more likely than those who don't to develop several types of cancer, including breast cancer, liver, rectum, mouth, throat and cancer of the esophagus, and that risk increases with increases in daily beverage alcohol consumption levels.

Richard W. Thatcher

Alcoholic Intoxication as a Chemical Killer

Attempts to ascertain specific benchmarks to identify the amount of alcohol ingestion that leads to death defy precision. A lethal dose of alcohol for 50 percent of the population is a blood alcohol level of approximately .50%, but deaths can occur at lower concentrations, and fail to occur at higher ones. Prediction of your own upper limits in this matter is a fool's game. The fact is that heavy drinking, especially very heavy drinking, is in most circumstances a sort of liquid version of Russian roulette.

Alcohol and Weight Problems

By the way, it is a myth that alcohol won't add to your weight problem. For one thing, young people who are drinking, who already have a greater sense of their invulnerability than grown-ups, tend to think that, when they drink, they should also finish off the evening during the wee hours with Chinese food or a pizza. Already feeling pretty unrestrained about satisfying their appetite for alcohol and fun, heavy drinkers, especially during their youthful years, treat food in the same way. Eventually, the pounds, almost inevitably, accumulate on our torsos, neck, arms and legs. All that "liquid fun" catches up with you

It is also true that alcohol itself is rich in calories (7 calories/gram) and has a major impact on the liver's ability to make fat. When alcohol is broken down in the liver, the liver is instructed, biochemically, to increase fat synthesis. Once fat is manufactured in the liver, it is distributed throughout the body to be stored in fat cells (adipose tissue). Thus, excessive drinking can produce a flabby, soft body because fat, also known as triglycerides, is stored in this adipose tissue when we consume more calories than we need to meet our body's energy needs. A pound of body fat is stored in this adipose tissue for every 3,500 calories that we drink. One ounce of alcohol actually supplies 210 calories, which scientists tell us is the equivalent of six teaspoons of lard. Now when rich mixes are added to liquor, and that late night pizza, the weight train just rolls through your body, leaving its fatty freight throughout.

Heavy Drinking and Water Retention

As concentration levels of alcohol increase in the blood, alcohol begins to inhibit what scientists refer to as the *antiduretic hormone* (ADH). This hormone normally functions to reabsorb water in the kidneys prior to elimination in the urine. Consequently, one's urine is more diluted and the fact that large amounts of liquid are typically being consumed at the time means that urination occurs in large volumes per episode or in frequent visits to the bathroom. Once blood alcohol concentrations have peaked, however, this copious discharge reverses. Water is retained in a condition, referred to as *antiduresis*, which results in swollen fingers, hands, and feet. Antiduresis is more pronounced if the drinker eats salty foods, such as snackers like salted peanuts or salty meal foods, while ingesting alcohol.

The inhibition of ADH during the drinking of alcoholic beverages can pose serious health risks. For example, long-distance runners, who lose a lot of water over the course of their run, can retain much higher doses of alcohol than s/he would otherwise and thus be vulnerable to rapid and extreme intoxication, depending on the dosage levels.

Effect on the Sleep Cycle

Despite the widespread belief that sleep can be induced with a "nightcap," after a quick hit of alcohol just before bedtime sleep patterns are actually affected adversely by alcohol Many problem drinkers and alcohol dependents report insomnia, a difficulty in getting to sleep or sleeping for a complete block of 6-8 hour time. Alcohol reduces the duration of rapid eye movement (REM) sleep. Depending on the dose of alcohol, REM sleep can be either partially or completely suppressed during the night, resulting in poor sleep and the unsettling experience of nightmares.

Hangovers

Approximately four to twelve hours after a bout of heavy drinking, and this is usually the next day, unpleasant symptoms of headache, nausea, fatigue, and thirst often occurs. As I'm sure you know, taken together, these symptoms are called a *hangover*–and it ain't pleasant!

Not everybody gets hangovers. Some people are spared. But there is research that suggests that at least one such experience is experienced by 40 percent of all men and 27 percent of all women over the age of eighteen.

It is believed that several factors together explain the hangover, but why its symptoms occur together to make the drinker suffer such discomfort is not known. I suppose it is remotely possible that it is nature's way to inform some of us that the night before we really crossed a line of dangerous toxicity when we drank–and we are foolish to cross it again. However, a hangover is also a state of mind that can be dangerous. The physical discomfort, mental dysfunction and frustration that so often accompanies a hangover leads to innumerable arguments and even fights between friends, lovers, spouses, and between students and teachers. This "tail end" of the over-drinking experience is legitimately located in the high risk column of any heavy drinking study.

Blackouts

You've heard of the *blackout*, of course. In fact, I expect that many of you will have experienced this charming phenomenon. A blackout involves a loss of memory of events that occurred in a specific period of one's most recent bout of intoxication. The events that seem to be erased from one's memory as a result of a blackout were consciously experienced at the time the individual was drinking.

It used to believe that blackouts only occur among older, long-time alcohol dependents. More recent research has made it clear that blackouts are also frequent in adolescents during drinking binges.

The probability of having a blackout is greatest when alcohol is consumed very quickly, forcing your blood alcohol level to rise very quickly— and there are several risk associated with blackouts. For one, you can be misled into thinking you said or did something you didn't or that something regrettable or humiliating that was said or done to you that wasn't.

Another risk with a blackout is that the drinker who has blackouts banks on his normal memory but, because of the hangover, that memory fails him the day after he wakes up from yesterday's drunk. I can personally remember waking up several times and not having a clue where I parked my car the night before. A lot of my acquaintances share memories of waking up not knowing where they are.

Wernicke-Korsakoff's Syndrome

Chronic alcohol use contributes to vitamin deficiencies, a condition referred to by physicians and biochemists as *avitaminosis*. This condition is caused either by a lack of adequate vitamin intake or an inability of the body to effectively use of available vitamins. When this condition occurs, over time, the body's reserves of many vitamins are depleted and a form of brain damage known as *Wernicke's encephalopathy* occurs. A direct result of thiamine deficiency – thiamin is one of a family of B vitamins – this syndrome results in the individual being disoriented and confused and also exhibiting abnormal eye movement. If untreated, most people suffering from this syndrome will go on to acquire *Korsakoff's psychosis*, sometimes referred to as *Korsakoff's syndrome*. Korsakoff's syndrome is a chronic brain syndrome in which the individual suffers from various thinking problems, including an inability to remember the past accurately and an inability to learn new information. The fact that Wernicke's encephalopathy so frequently leads to Korsakoff's syndrome has united the names in the common scientific references to the occurrence of both syndromes: *Wernicke-Korsakoff's Syndrome*.

Alcohol's Effect on the State of Human Emotions

As I've noted above, alcohol is a central nervous system (CNS) depressant. As a depressant, it is remarkably effective. Some research has indicated that the depressant effects from just a single drink can last 96 hours. The effects of an alcohol binge of 1 or 2 days might last for several weeks during a period of abstinence that occurs after the binge.

It is hardly a secret that alcohol affect's one's emotional and mental condition in various ways, from impairing perception, thinking capacity and judgement, to exaggerating or bringing to the surface various feelings, from sadness to rage. The results of these later combinations of drugs and emotions are so well known that they needn't be repeated.

Drinking and Suicide

While no cause-effect relationship has been established between alcohol and suicide, the available research does suggest that alcohol is a contributing factor in many suicides. The fact that alcohol reduces human inhibitions, existing thoughts about suicide or self-destructive behaviour generally may be more likely to be translated into action. Ongoing emotional frustrations or mental illness, such as paranoia or depression, which can lead to suicidal thoughts, may also be more likely to be enacted when heavy drinking occurs by individuals with these conditions.

Drinking, High Risk Sex and Partner Abuse

Mixing alcohol and sexual relations is laden with many risks. Under the influence of alcohol, both men and women are more likely to be violent with their partners. A study of men charged with battering their intimate partners found that at the time of the incident, 60% of them were under the influence of alcohol.

Two-thirds of the violent crimes committed by a current or former spouse or intimate partner report that alcohol was a factor in the violent episode. Other studies based on self-reports estimate that alcohol is involved in 75% of spousal abuse incidents.

An estimated 30% of child abuse cases in the United States are thought to involve alcohol consumption episodes. Some estimates suggest that figure is closer to 40%.

The fact that alcohol consumption lowers the inhibitions of drinkers means that after several glasses, the drinkers are more likely to try to act out their sexual urges. For males this tends to increase the aggressiveness regarding sexual goals and, for females, this often means a greater willingness to accept the encouragement of males. While having sex or not having sex are in part simply moral choices, those choices have practical implications. For both males and females, this greater permissiveness often means that sexual intercourse is conducted *without* appropriate protection, whether condoms or birth control pills. The result can be an unwanted pregnancy, which tends to lead to substantially reduced opportunities in life for both the mother and her offspring. The result can also be a venereal disease or HIV/AIDS, the latter of which, despite great advances in medication, remains a physically damaging and sometimes lethal syndrome.

When the thinking of a girl is impaired by alcohol, she is more likely to miss cues that would normally signal the possibility of an imminent sexual assault. That tendency to miss cues all too often combines with the expectations and lowered inhibitions of males after drinking to lead to rape. With startling frequency, "date rape" is an outcome of heavy drinking by females in contact with unscrupulous males.

Alcohol and Pregnancy

Alcohol also poses major risks for the unborn babies inside pregnant mothers, whatever their ages. Many expectant mothers are already aware that indulging in too much alcohol during pregnancy can result in Fetal Alcohol Spectrum Disorder (formerly simply referred to as Fetal Alcohol Syndrome).

An abundance of studies have shown that alcohol consumed during pregnancy produces specific birth defects in offspring by disrupting fetal development, even when differences in the quality of a child's nutrition are taken into account.

Later in life, FASD children show deficits in short-term memory and problem-solving ability. Many also display hyperactivity in school and difficulty in forming a solidified pattern of moral judgement. Research has shown problems in learning and memory among adolescents, both black and white, whose mothers drank during pregnancy.

At the extreme end of the spectrum, FASD children show other indications of limited mental ability and a characteristic skull and facial appearance that include a smaller-than-normal head, small, wide-set eyes, drooping eyelids, a flattening of the vertical groove between the mouth and nose, a thin upper lip and a short, upturned nose. Most children affected by the syndrome only exhibit some of these characteristics, however.

One of the greatest sources of risk for FASD is the pregnancy associated with unplanned sexual activity. When sexual activity leading to pregnancy occurs in the absence of any birth control protection, the female who conceives will typically be unaware of her pregnancy for a full month. During that time many will drink from one more time to many drinking episodes in which many drinks are consumed during each drinking episode.

Unfortunately, there is no clear evidence regarding exactly how much alcohol will predictably result in FASD. So until more is known, any drinking of alcoholic beverages by a female who knows she is pregnant or even if she simply thinks she is pregnant is clearly ill-advised. In other words, as far as researchers know, there is no safe threshold for the amount of alcohol that can safely be consumed during a pregnancy.

Alcohol's Reactions with Other Drugs

Another set of negative effects of alcohol is its complex interactions with other drugs. Studies of emergency room patient intakes reveal that both the incidence of medical crises and deaths in hospital emergency rooms are especially high for patients admitted who have combined alcohol with either prescribed medications or street drugs. The benefits of prescribed medications are often reduced because of the use of alcohol. Consider the following:

- Having a few drinks with other depressant drugs, sometimes known as "downers," is especially dangerous. Well–known drugs in this class include tranquillizers and sleeping pills. The alcohol and the other drug "boost" each other's effects. The result can be that a person may seem very drunk, quite unexpectedly, and can pass out or go into a coma, even die. When alcohol is coupled with such non-prescription drugs as antihistamines, which are commonly taken for colds or allergies, a person can become dopey and clumsy.

- Taking stimulant drugs such as cocaine, caffeine or amphetamines during or after drinking a lot of alcohol can trick you into thinking you are sober. In fact, you may well be simply more wide awake and more hyper (i.e., hyper-aroused).

- Some medicines can't do their job as well if they are mixed with alcohol, while other medicines can interact violently with alcohol, causing side effects such as vomiting, headaches, and cramps.

The Costs of Heavy Drinking for Society

Someday you'll probably be a tax-paying member of society – and maybe you are already – and, when or if you now are, you are likely to care a great deal about the costs of social problems and health problems to society as a whole—and their costs to you as a taxpayer. So let's consider the financial impact of alcohol problems on the public coffers.

A 2001 study based on a national household survey in the United States found that approximately 109 million Americans aged 12 and over currently drink alcohol. Approximately 12.9 million of those current drinkers admit to being "heavy drinkers," which means that, on average, they had been drinking, at least 5 drinks per day in the previous 30 days. In the same study, one-fifth of the population 12 and over engaged in binge drinking during the 30 days prior to when they were surveyed. The study was conducted by the U.S. Substance Abuse and Mental Health Services Administration and is referred to as the National Household Survey on Drug Abuse.

Economic Costs of Heavy Drinking

You may not yet be an income tax payer yet but when you are, the financial price of heavy drinking will hit your wallet like brick.

The direct and indirect financial costs of alcohol abuse in the United States and Canada are astronomical. Estimates of these costs are typically calculated on a yearly basis and include loss of productivity in the workplace, work lost by victims of alcohol-related accidents and crimes, health care, and the incarceration (jailing) of criminals.

According to the National Institute on Alcohol Abuse and Alcoholism (NIAAA), in recent years, alcohol abuse costs in the United States hover around $185 billion. Approximately $26 billion, or 14% of the total, comes from direct medical costs or treating alcoholics. Almost half — a whopping $88 billion — comes from lost productivity. It must be admitted that these figures are not counterbalanced by estimates of various benefits, however—and they have been criticised as being inflated, based on their accounting assumptions. Whatever the accuracy or inaccuracy of these figures, the costs are enormous.

Amongst other things, people who drink too much and too often are at greater risk for diabetes and several kinds of cancer, according to some studies—and these health problems are now among the major drivers of health care cost increases, both in terms of individual and public costs.

A Canadian study commissioned by the Centre for Addictions and Mental Health in Toronto, estimated that, in 2002, alcohol problems cost every Canadian just over $460 per year and just over $1700 per family.

Alcohol Abuse is Strongly Implicated in Serious Crimes

I've discussed violence and drinking in relation to intimate partners but alcohol is implicated in various, serious crimes. Again, this is hardly a surprise.

Over-drinking does not *cause* serious crime but it is so strongly associated with it that the relationship between the two has to be considered a huge public health concern and its very nature demands a careful examination.

A 1998 U.S. Department of Justice report that compiled statistics on criminal prosecutions reported that nearly 4 in 10 violent victimizations involved the use of alcohol. The same summary indicated that alcohol use was implicated in about 4 in 10 fatal motor vehicle accidents. The summary also indicated that about 4 in 10 criminal offenders, regardless of whether they are on probation, in local jail, or in State prison, self-reported that they were using alcohol at the time of the offense for which they were convicted. Previous studies had indicated that approximately two-thirds of those convicted of threats to the public order did so while under the influence of alcohol. Those "threats to the public order" included weapons offenses, obstruction of justice, traffic offenses, and driving while drinking,

Drinking is a common factor in assaults and injuries caused by assaultive battery resulting in death, especially in the case of adolescents and young adults. Drinking cannot be viewed as an actual *cause* of assaultive behaviour but, when taken together, the many factors involved in an episode of physical violence among drinkers can be taken as a strong influence. Drinking and assaults and drinking and killing tend to go together far more often than most people realize. Several studies have shown that, in the United States, approximately 60% of all murders are committed when the killer was drinking.

Heavy Drinking Norms Diminish the Quality of Community Life

When widespread, heavy drinking becomes a norm in a community, the general quality of life in that community can descend to a level that makes business avoid that community for investment purposes and makes existing businesses abandon the community. The people in the community increasingly live in fear of the entire menu of craziness that attends widespread, heavy drinking norms: additional substance abuse problems, spousal abuse, child neglect, violence, theft, street muggings, shootings, knifings, and a general despair associated with living in fear of ugly, negative outcomes. Granted, it is usually economic and social factors that encourage and reinforce heavy drinking norms, but those norms can themselves be a drag on community vitality leading to economic problems. In addition, once those norms are established, additional, serious social and personal problems reach a sort of "take-off" stage which, once arrived at, an entire chain of additional social problems and health problems appear.

Alcohol's Ugly Relationship with Human Accidents and Injuries

Many alcohol-related health troubles are more immediate and they are delivered with a crash, a thud or a bang. Half of the trauma patients in emergency rooms got there because they hurt themselves after drinking. The professions where people drink the most include construction, agriculture and manufacturing—all fields that involve a lot of dangerous, heavy machinery.

Drinking and Driving

While we're on the subject of injuries, we have to consider drinking and driving. When it comes to youth injuries and premature deaths, drinking and driving (DUI: 'Driving Under the Influence) is the biggest culprit of all.

There is really no question that the consumption of alcohol significantly impairs one's ability to drive or skilfully navigate traffic. In 1999, of the 41,480 traffic fatalities recorded in the United States, 38% involved an intoxicated driver with a BAC level of 0.10 or more and 50% showing a BAC level of 0.05 percent. What may even further jar you into the risks of drinking and driving is the fact that in that same year, 60 percent of teenagers who died in automobile crashes had been drinking prior to the crash.

> For many males, to have someone else take one's car keys or make commanding statements about *not* driving while impaired, are both perceived as a threat to their sense of masculinity. In far too many instances, that dismissive statement, "I'm fine. No one's gonna tell me whether I can drive or not," has proven to be "famous last words."

When BAC levels are beyond 0.15 percent, the risks of having an automobile accident are 380 times higher than driving without any alcohol in your blood. Even when BAC levels are only between .02 and .04, the risk of having a car accident are 48 times greater. By any accounts, these are very sobering facts.

It is worth noting that a person in a motor vehicle accident is also likely to have a more serious set of injuries if they have been drinking than if they have not been drinking. Both drivers and passengers who have been drinking are 4 times more likely to die in the accident if they have been drinking than if they have not had any drinks. This is probably best explained by the fact that heavy drinking leads to increased bleeding in the spinal cord and increased swelling in brain tissue, which slows down the flow of life-sustaining oxygen needed by the brain.

Lowered inhibitions increase with drink and, when inhibitions are reduced, human judgement is diminished and an individual is more prone to take greater than usual risks.

When people are impaired by alcohol, they are also less likely to resist the encouragement of others to avoid taking risks, such as driving a car when inebriated. For many males, a personal sense of manhood is threatened by someone who takes one's car keys away or makes commanding statements about *not* driving while impaired. In far too many instances a statement like, "Hell with it, I'm alright to drive!", has proven to be those "famous last words."

Another impairing effect of drinking that has implications for reduced driving capacity is the relaxation of the muscles of the eye and the resulting blurring of vision. There are three muscles responsible for manipulating the eye in a way that facilitates visual perception. These ciliary muscles work together and, when an individual has a bout of heavy drinking, their coordinated functioning is diminished. As a result, the eyes relax, and blurred vision is the upshot.

The reduced muscular coordination in the eyes also lowers one's capacity to react effectively to glare. Thus, when one is inebriated, the glare from headlights of oncoming cars results in a delay in the recovery of clear visual perception. This means that the eyes are unable to provide the impaired driver with the type of information about the location of the car on the road that is required to drive safely.

> **Both drivers and passengers who have been drinking are 4 times more likely to die in the accident if they have been drinking than if they have not had any drinks. This is probably best explained by the fact that heavy drinking leads to increased bleeding in the spinal cord and increased swelling in brain tissue.**

When people drink and drive at night, their visual perception declines substantially. When streetlights are not in place, the reduction can be as much as 80% of normal vision.

Dealing with other drunk drivers on the road is a problem for sober drivers. Obviously, defensive driving is a much more challenging task for drivers who are themselves impaired by too many drinks.

In short, widespread problem prinking seriously undermines the quality of life in communities–and taxpayers and public service workers have to pay for picking up the pieces after the damage is done. Fortunately, by imposing legal BAC level limits, typically of .08, accidents involving intoxicated drivers have been significantly reduced in recent years. Thousands of lives have been saved through this legislation.

You should know that some jurisdictions are now converting their laws to even lower levels, reducing the legal limit of drinking before driving to one bottle of beer or its equivalent. Such a limit is now the law in the Canadian, west coast province of British Columbia. Many other Canadian provinces and American states are looking seriously at the British Columbia example as an option because fatality rates for motor vehicle accidents in that province have fallen significantly since the introduction of the more stringent limits.

Chapter 6

Types of Stinkin' Drinkin'

I'd like you to consider the variety of alcohol problems that are common in North America. I'm going to begin with the definitions given by psychiatrists and then move on to the observations of others, including some of my own.

Psychiatric Diagnoses of Alcohol Problems

Most scientists now distinguish between simple problem drinking and alcohol dependency (still commonly referred to as "alcoholism" by the general public and many Counsellors, or "chronic stage, habitual problem drinking" by some professionals). Alcoholism, a term that is being rejected by many addictions professionals today, has been defined as human behaviour disorder by the World Health Organization (WHO). In its written materials, the WHO itself has formally replaced the term alcoholism with the term "alcohol-dependence syndrome."

Alcohol Dependence (i.e., 'Alcohol Addiction' or 'Alcoholism')

The WHO definition of alcohol dependency suggests that drinking is a problem that can be described in terms of three factors:

1. the degree to which a person's drinking behaviour is abnormal;

2. the degree to which the drinker feels there is something wrong with their drinking; or

3. the degree to which the drinker has acquired an altered physiological response to alcohol (tolerance and withdrawal symptoms).

The American Psychiatric Association now uses the term "alcohol dependence," which it once referred to as alcoholism, in a somewhat similar fashion to the definition given by the World Health Organization. The diagnostic desk manual for psychiatrists is referred to by its shorthand "DSM" (the current version is the 'DSM-IV,' and the next, soon to be out, version, will be the 'DSM-V'), which stands for the "Diagnostic and Statistical Manual." The manual has been adopted in its several, updated versions by the American Psychiatric Association (the APA). For the most part, clinical psychologists also use the APA manual. Once utilizing the term "alcoholism," recent versions of the DSM have substituted the term "alcohol dependency," which it describes as follows:

> A maladaptive pattern of substance use, leading to clinically significant impairment or distress, as manifested by three (or more) of the following, occurring at any time in the same 12-month period:

1. tolerance, as defined by either of the following:

    (a) a need for markedly increased amounts of alcohol to achieve intoxication or desired effect

    (b) markedly diminished effect with continued use of the same amount of the substance

2. withdrawal, as manifested by (a) either of the following:

    i. the development of an alcohol-specific syndrome due to the cassation of (or reduction) in alcohol use that has been heavy and prolonged

    ii. the alcohol-specific syndrome causes clinically significant distress or impairment in social, occupational, or other important areas of functioning; and

    (b) alcohol or another drug substituting for alcohol is used to relieve or avoid withdrawal symptoms

3. the substance is often taken in larger amounts or over a longer period than was intended

4. there is a persistent desire or unsuccessful efforts to cut down or control substance use

5. a great deal of time is spent in activities necessary to obtain the substance (e.g., driving long distances), use the substance (e.g., serial drinking), or recover from its effects

6. important social, occupational, or recreational activities are given up or reduced because of substance use

7. the substance use is continued despite knowledge of having a persistent or recurrent physical or psychological problem that is likely to have been caused or exacerbated by alcohol consumption (e.g., continued drinking despite recognition that an ulcer was made worse by alcohol consumption).

The DSM-IV manual goes on to indicate that alcohol dependence can involve either or both physiological dependence, which entails an increased tolerance for alcohol and withdrawal symptoms when not drinking, and psychological dependence, in which there is no evidence of tolerance or withdrawal.

The manual also suggests measures of remission (recovery) from alcohol dependence. These include *early full remission* (total abstinence after treatment for a period ranging from 1 to 11 months after treatment and *early partial remission*, which allows for minor episodes of relapse during a period ranging from 1 to 11 months. It also includes *sustained full remission*, which runs beyond 12 months and *partial sustained remission*, a condition which includes sustained abstinence with occasional bouts of relapse after a 12-month period.

For those afflicted by alcohol dependency, there are a series of typical risks. Those risks include many of the negative consequences from drinking that I have already described, as well as several others. They include:

- permanently damaged family and marital relationships;
- loss of friendships;

- education and job losses;
- residential instability and, in its extreme form, homelessness;
- a high probability of frequent conflict with the law;
- loss of driving privileges;
- substantially increased personal safety risks;
- beatings, bullying, muggings; and
- death from beatings, exposure to the elements and fires.

Problems also associated with alcohol dependency include a host of physical health problems, from cirrhosis of the liver, high risks of alcoholic poisoning, and mental impairment. Alcohol dependency is also implicated as a risk for various devastating illnesses related to the combined concentration of poverty and close physical interaction among those with high health risks. Such illnesses include HIV/AIDS, Hepatitis B and C, and, increasingly, a renewed wave of Tuberculosis among disadvantaged populations.

Non-alcoholic Problem Drinking (Alcohol Abuse): The Elephant in the Room that Society Tends to Ignore

Despite its overwhelming and often tragic impact, alcoholism does not account for the majority of problems associated with alcohol consumption in North America today. Why? Because the sheer numbers of people who occasionally get drunk and the numbers of people who exhibit a problematic drinking style far outnumber alcohol dependents.

While even the most ambitious estimates of the percentage of alcoholics in the North American population place the figure below 10 percent, between one-quarter and one-third of the population aged 12 years and older report drinking 5 or more drinks on at least one occasion in the past month. If everyone 12 years of age or older were asked if they have ever been drunk, the numbers would certainly swell to well over half the population and some have speculated the figure would climb as high as 75 percent of the population.

Thinkin' Drinkin'

Problem drinking or what I have called "stinkin' drinkin'" is a drinking style that occurs occasionally rather than frequently and with regularity, does not involve physical or psychological dependency but does involve heavy drinking, often with intoxication being one of the primary goals of the drinking episode. In turn, many of those drunken episodes lead to problems of a magnitude that ranges from a very limited to an extremely major human cost.

While one such episode can sensibly be described as alcohol abuse, when psychiatrists use the term they are referring to a *pattern* of such abuse or, in other words, a recurring part of an individual's lifestyle.

According to the American Psychiatric Association (AMA), *alcohol abuse* is defined in the DSM-IV as follows:

> a maladaptive pattern of alcohol use leading to clinically significant impairment or distress, as manifested by one (or more) of the following, occurring within a 12-month period:
>
> (1) recurrent substance use resulting in failure to fulfill major role obligations at work, school, or home (e.g. repeated absences or poor work performance related to alcohol abuse; alcohol-related suspensions or expulsions from school; neglect of children or household)
>
> (2) recurrent alcohol abuse in situations in which it is physically hazardous (e.g., driving an automobile or operating a machine when impaired by alcohol use)
>
> (3) recurrent alcohol-related legal problems (e.g., arrests for alcohol-related disorderly conduct)
>
> (4) continued alcohol use despite having persistent or recurrent social or interpersonal problems caused by exacerbated by the effects of alcohol (e.g., arguments with an intimate partner about the consequences of intoxication, physical fights.

In its clinical definition, the DSM-IV manual adds that the classification of substance (alcohol or other mood-modifying drug) abuse supersedes alcohol dependence if the individual's symptoms have never met the criteria for alcohol abuse.

When you read this definition, don't forget to read it carefully. If you think a problem drinker must meet several or *all* of the listed criteria, think again. The definition is clear: It is *one or more* of the four symptoms. The more you exhibit, of course, or the more intense any one of the symptoms, the greater is your problem and the more important it is to take stock of your situation and, probably, get immediate assistance from a Counsellor. You will also notice that the distinction between the two gets a little blurred when you look at some of the "softer" criteria the DSM-IV assigns to alcohol dependency.

Negative outcomes of alcohol abuse can also include many of the problems associated with alcohol dependency, like destroyed love relationships and sullied trust and feelings of emotional closeness with parents and friends. Teachers insulted at school dances and employers "set straight" by employees giving drunken expression to "real feelings" at staff parties are frequent victims of the scornful utterances of the occasional drunk. Often, no one is the winner in these exchanges because these personal attacks often lead to retaliation, resulting in such losses to the drinker as school suspensions or firings or demotions at work—and more often than not, the person delivering the insult regrets having done so after the fact.

As a Public Policy Concern, the Problem Drinking of Non-Alcoholics has Been a Very Low Priority

As I've noted above, compared with alcohol dependency and other drug addictions, non-addicted problem drinking gets relatively little press or public policy attention. Also as I've noted, this may be explained by the fact that drunken episodes are so very much a routine aspect of North American culture and so prevalent in our society.

Alcohol dependency (alcoholism) is certainly a real and extremely challenging health problem, so I will therefore devote specific attention to alcoholism in a subsequent chapter.

It is true that problem drinking has been a source of considerable public attention in one area, namely drinking and driving, and this concern has resulted in extensive legislative change and expanded regulation. Unfortunately, this exception proves the rule that compared with alcoholism, problem drinking gets very little concerted attention by policy makers and the media and press that reports on the issue. The prevention of alcoholism and "rehabilitation" for alcoholics consumes most of the focus of policy makers, mental health and "addictions" Counsellors, and treatment program time.

In turn, various illicit "street drugs" and inappropriately used prescription drug use draw an enormous amount of attention from policy makers and, in turn the press and media. In fact, the U.S. federal government regards what it calls the "War on Drugs" a national public policy priority. Admittedly, these problems carry enormous risks and huge challenges for youth, policy makers, social workers, and police. Illicit drugs, including heroin, cocaine, amphetamine and new, designer drugs tend to get the lion's share of press and media exposure. The illegal drug trade in all its dimensions garners enormous interest in the media, whether through the reporting of public policy discussions and debates or in radio, television and Internet talk forums or dramatic entertainment presented in television shows and movies.

By comparison, there is very limited media and press attention given to drinking binges by non-alcoholics. It is true that drunken binges as a factor in crimes or family conflicts continues to be an occasional aspect of many if not most dramatic series but, compared with illicit "street" or prescription drugs, the attention is minimal. What news we do hear about binge drinking tends to be restricted to drinking and driving issues and the implications of drunken behaviour in rioting after major sports events or through the occasional reporting of

> **Most alcohol related health and social problems occur whether the people with the drinking problem are alcoholics or simply problem drinkers. However, there are a lot more problem drinkers than there are alcoholics and everyone who gets drunk is at least a one-time problem drinker and a potential repeater.**

a new scientific study or poll—and that attention is brief and very quickly bumped from the stage of public discussion.

Most alcohol related health and social problems occur whether the people with the drinking problem are alcoholics or simply problem drinkers. However, there are a lot more problem drinkers than alcoholics and, if you think about it, everyone who gets drunk is at least a one-time problem drinker and a potential repeater.

The public interest in drugs rather than booze may be partially explained by the fact that illicit seem more exotic, and there always seems to be a new substance in the underground market—and that's newsworthy itself. It may also be partially explained by the fact that the sale and use of "street" drugs or diverted prescription drugs is illegal and thus associated with organized crime, while much of the alcohol trade is legalized. And the U.S. federal government's "War on Drugs" is primarily focussed on erasing the illegal drug trade and its tragic outcomes. So, aside from the problem of chronic alcoholism and these other issues, just drinking too much is really not even on the radar screen for those paid to worry about or write or broadcast about health and social problems.

So in public policy discourse just plain old alcohol abuse is given short shrift. It is as if the problem is simply a given, an inevitable part of life, a fixture of human society that will never go away. We don't even think about it as an abiding concern. Yet we should think about it, talk about it, and do something about it, as individuals, families, communities and as nations, because its nasty consequences are legion.

Binge Drinking

Drinking in binges is the most common form of problem drinking. More than one in four U.S. teens and young adults admit they are binge drinkers, health officials said Tuesday.

In the United States, **BINGE DRINKING is defined as having four or more drinks for women, and five or more drinks for men, over a couple of hours.** These numbers are different because men and women metabolize alcohol differently.

Clearly, it is not just teens that are affected. According to the report from the U.S. Centers for Disease Control and Prevention (CDC), more than 33 million adults have reported binge drinking in the past year.

According to the director of the Centers for Disease Control, Dr. Thomas R. Frieden, "Binge drinking is a very large health and social problem and one that has gone largely unnoticed." In a news conference on Tuesday, October 11, 2011, Dr. Frieden commented: "Most people who binge drink are not alcoholic. It may be because binge drinking has not been recognized as a problem [that] it has not decreased in the past 15 years."

Heavy drinking in binges can lead to a wide range of very serious personal problems of a social, psychological, emotional and physical (health) nature. It also imposes enormous costs on society.

It is critical to understand that many, if not most, of these problems occur whether the people with the drinking problem are alcoholics or simply problem drinkers. However, the fact is that there are a lot more problem drinkers than alcoholics and, it is possible to argue that, everyone who gets drunk at least once is an occasional problem drinker. This means that the majority of North Americans over the age of 12 years old are implicated in the destructive side of alcohol use.

> **You should know that drinking can justifiably be considered a 'gateway' drug, especially when you start regular use when you are very young.**

It is worth considering the fact that problem drinking is also a "gateway" to other forms substance of abuse—a gate which, for the individual experimenting with or frequently engaged in heavy drinking, is far more likely to be opened to experimentation with other drugs and, potentially, to addiction. Once the gate swings open to excessive drinking for an individual, especially if it is opened at a young age, the chances increase substantially that the same individual will try other mood-modifying drugs, from the relatively benign marijuana to a host of other more dangerous drugs. It should also be noted that the available research on the subject indicates that the chances that you will try additional drugs seems to increase more with each new drug you try.

The research is also pretty clear that problem drinking and drug use, both independently or taken together, increase your chances of partaking in a lot of other activities that can have pretty troublesome long-term consequences. As I've noted above – and as you will not be surprised to hear – these include acts of violence and various forms of troublesome behaviour, such as unprotected sex, unplanned pregnancies, theft and vandalism.

The mere fact that there are so many more problem drinkers and occasional binge drinkers than there are alcoholics, makes it clear that the societal costs of non-dependent, problem drinking far outweigh the aggregated costs of alcohol dependency.

Common Types of Non-Alcoholic, Problem Drinkers: Some Personal Observations

In my opinion, it is important to have a closer look at this non-dependent, problem drinker concept, at least by breaking it down into some of the "garden variety" types which, in varying degrees, create irritants or pose serious problems for themselves or others.

1. The 'Garden Variety,' Annoying and Embarrassing Drunk (AED). This type of alcohol abuser is quite common. You run into them at every other party or bar you visit on occasion. This is the person who acts up, whether through extreme, demonstrative behaviour (the lamp shade wearing life of the party). the slobbering, overly sentimental conversationalist, or the person who insists on sharing in unwanted detail his achievements, the sad things in his personal life, or betraying the confidences of others.. It is also the regretful gossip, the person who confides the closest secrets of others and then finds herself ashamed and distrusted after the drinking session. I call this type of drinker the annoying and embarrassing drunk and they seem to be a very common type indeed.

Sub-Types of AEDs that I Have Encountered

There is a plurality of eccentric patterns that have proven troublesome for those who drink beverage alcohol. I have personally noticed a variety of behaviour patterns that emerge with some consistency when people drink:

- the "sad sack," who seems to have stored up all his or her emotional aches and pains and decides that a drinking session is a time to share them all;

- the sentimental sop or "maudlin drinker" as I call him (or her), who becomes uncharacteristically and excessively sentimental;

- the argumentative drinker who just can't contain his or her temptation to aggressively challenge the opinion of anyone who shares a fact or idea;

- the hideaway drinker: the person who successfully conceals a persistent habit, drinking alone and hiding bottles from family members;

- the loudmouth who considers himself an entertainer as soon as four drinks have been soaked up (whom, for every chuckle triggered, emits three or four insensitive, vulgar or just plain not funny lines);

- the promiscuous (or 'sexaholic') drinker who assertively seeks out and engages in sex as an essential element, if not the exclusive motivation, for drinking;

- the gossip, who shares the details, whether real or imagined, of other peoples' lives. This is often accompanied by the betrayal of confidence gained from others.

No doubt, through experience, you have also assembled such a cast of characters in your memory.

Of the types of AED drinking personalities I have identified above, you may fit readily into one or you may take on elements of more than one of them—and you may take on one of these patterns at different degrees of intoxication. Nailing down all of them might have some value but of more interest is trying to understand *how* variation in drinking results in varying levels of risk.

2. The Occasional, Disastrous Drunk. Any time one becomes intoxicated, the risks for disaster of various types increase. This type therefore includes everyone who over-indulges and, at least on occasion, gets so "plastered" that they do really careless and very stupid things... Think about it, though. One bad drunk can make you and unplanned-for-parent, a perpetrator of violence that lands you in jail, or a maimed or dead driver or passenger in a car, truck, all-terrain vehicle or boat driven by somebody who is drunk. So I give this type of drinker the *Occasional, Disastrous Drunk*. Such high risk drinking behaviour, however occasional, can also result – and all too often does — in unwanted pregnancies and the complicated burdens that circumstance brings to mothers (and sometimes fathers) and their children, as well as a serious, sex-related illness acquired because of a lack of protection during the heated throes of unprotected sex.

3. The Normal Guy/Gal, Bad Drunk. This *normal guy/gal, bad drunk* type of drinker normally displays an unremarkable, relatively balanced personality and does usually does not drink on a frequent or regular basis, yet when s/he does drink, s/he often acts out in a flamboyant, bizarre and often high risk fashion. These individuals exhibit troubling communications of either a hostile or bizarre nature. They also typically display modestly self-destructive and/or anti-social behaviour during drinking episodes. This type of drinker does not have *severe* psychological problems, however, and will typically return to relatively normal behaviour after the drinking and hangover have passed. The normal-but–acting-out-when-drunk does tend to reflect some troubling, underlying psychological or social frustrations, however, and the behaviour should be considered a signal that some things need to be addressed. The pattern is often driven by unresolved emotional issues and problems of social adjustment, such as low self-esteem, shyness is social gatherings, and may include moderate but, persistent anger or ongoing anxieties of other kinds, mild depression or other underlying psychological challenges. Such bad drinking behaviour can also simply be a learned habit that was acquired by role modeling and participation with family or close friends during early adolescence—a pattern that has been inadvertently reinforced by others showing affection for these individuals by giving them special attention in the form of expressions of endearment or finding great humour in their antics. For these people, drinking is clearly not a useful way of addressing their psychic conflicts or even just behaving, and such reinforcement is ill-advised.

4. The Predictably Destructive Drinker. There is also a type of drinker who does not become addicted to alcohol but whose drinking episodes are made destructive by serious, underlying personality disorders of a chronic type. These include such major disorders anti-social personality disorder, clinical depression or bipolar disorder (dramatic mood swings between depression and hyperactive emotional expression). Like the alcoholic, the personality-disordered person who sometimes drinks heavily should be encouraged to seek out professional, therapeutic help to deal with the motivational issues that are resulting in the dangerous drinking pattern. This type of drinker is the most dangerous of all, whether to self or others. Amongst them, the anti-social drinker, is the most dangerous of all because he (and it is usually a he) often turns to predatory behaviour or other types of behaviour while under the influence of alcohol. The depressed and bipolar drinker can place themselves at high risk of self-destructive, sometimes suicidal, behaviour, and others as for acted out rage or bizarre interactions. If you fit into this pattern, don't delay, walk, no run, to a clinical psychologist, physician or substance abuse Counsellor and get the help you desperately need.

Whether your issue is one of alcohol addiction or a non-addictive, stinkin' drinkin' behaviour pattern, you should address the problem four square. If you care at all for your own health and safety, you ABSOLUTELY *MUST* address the problem.

Individuals with troubling drinking patterns often feel pressured by professional (and non-professional) problem drinking advisors – Counsellors and alcohol educators – to accept the alcoholic label if they are to participate in treatment.. In my opinion, that very pressure is typically better mischief than aid, however good the intentions of the helping person. I know I experienced many problems with drinking, but in looking back, I think I feared the alcoholic label and that fear repelled me from seeking out the ear of a wise Counsellor or even getting down to business and addressing my own problem.

Make sure you do get screened for the type of problem drinking you are afflicted with. If it is clear that you are alcohol dependent, then a program aimed at abstinence is essential to your health and well-being. If you are not alcohol dependent, then what you need is training in sensible, moderate drinking—and if you want to do it on your own, it is all here, in the final chapters of this book.

If an individual can learn responsible drinking behaviour, which essentially means LIMITING THE AMOUNT that he or she drinks and NOT ENGAGING IN CARELESS OR ANTI-SOCIAL BEHAVIOUR *when* drinking, then, essentially they have conquered the problem. So why should that person be subjected to the humiliating process by which individuals are labelled "alcoholics forever," intimate confessionals are demanded, total abstinence is deemed essential, and self-help group involvement is considered requisite?

At the risk of too much repetition, *most* alcohol-related problems are not the result of an addiction to alcohol, despite the stubborn beliefs of many alcohol educators and Counsellors.

It is also true that many factors, including inherited genes and social pressures do result in alcohol addiction for a minority of people and, truly, this often becomes both a chronic psychological and medical disorder that desperately demands intense treatment.—and a life course strategy of abstinence and avoiding people and situations that trigger the relapse of drinking behaviour.

You Don't Have to 'Bottom Out': Address Your Drinking Problems *Now*

It may be conceded that for most people it takes a bit of a wake-up call to make them think about starting to address a troubling or drinking pattern. For some, it takes a loud, screamingly loud, wake-up call. But I simply can't accept that this "turning point" has to be the type of devastating experience that AA advocates seem to think must occur before one starts taking one's problem seriously. In fact, the balance of reputable research does not support the view that we have to "bottom out" before we can overcome our alcohol problem. And as I've noted, the research that I've examined seems to be on my side.

If you think about it, the concept of bottoming out is itself pretty shaky. Just as it's a true that you can always run into somebody tougher than you or smarter than you, you can also always confront a set of circumstances that are worse than\what you have experienced in the past. In other words, short of death, there can always be a deeper bottom.

So a significant turning point is probably inevitable in your confrontation with your drinking problem, but that may simply involve reading this book. It might also simply be an intimate, a friend or parent telling you it's time to wise up before you find yourself in a little more trouble than you can handle.

I believe that the chances are all on your side if you want to sensibly manage your drinking throughout your life—at least from here on. You do have to make a clear commitment to either abstinence or moderate drinking, however. You also have to wisely substitute practical and emotionally satisfying things for whatever it is you derive from heavy drinking. And yes, there is increasing evidence to support this view.

But no, you don't have "hit bottom" before getting serious about addressing a drinking problem. That very idea may be the cruellest

> **You don't have to admit to being an 'alcoholic' simply because you are experiencing a drinking problem. Chances are you're not an alcoholic but it is vitally important that you take the drinking problem seriously.**

and most wrong-headed of principles coming out of the treatment industry in the past half century. The fact is that you can simply use your noggin and act immediately, guided by the recognition that unmanaged, unguided, careless drinking is dangerous as hell. Even one episode is dangers and the more such binges occur, the greater the risk.

A book by Anne M. Fletcher was based on interviews with individuals who had overcome alcohol problems. In her research for the book, *Sober for Good*, published in 2001, Fletcher found that a large minority of these people, all of whom described themselves as "alcoholics," did not have to experience devastating personal circumstances associated with their drinking before they addressed the problem. They did have to convince themselves, however, that the short-term pleasures of heavy drinking were not worth the negative consequences they often experienced as a result.

It is also worth noting that current research suggests that any positive intervention, especially the help of family and friends or professional Counsellors, can produce positive benefits for an individual with an alcohol problem, no matter how intense their motivation at the time.

In fairness, while AA literature suggests that you probably have to hit bottom before you begin to change – which means that you have experienced a major catastrophe related to your drinking or losing almost everything that is dear to you – it also suggests that some people can commit to recovery without such profound circumstances.

Many treatment professionals and AA spokespersons believe that if a problem drinker is to have any chance of benefiting from treatment s/he must admit to self-identification as an alcoholic. Presumably, you either are or you aren't an alcoholic. If you aren't, the label is nothing but a burden and an excuse for not managing your own affairs effectively. That very idea is extremely wrong-headed in my opinion. It encourages those who think they might be an alcoholic to use this alleged "disease" or "weakness" as an excuse for getting drunk all the time. On the other hand, it scares many people away from getting help if they think they just might be an alcoholic. Frozen in denial, they keep putting the matter off. And most of you are simply not alcoholics and, if you act sensibly now, it is unlikely that you will ever become one.

The important thing about a drinking problem is that you must address it, and do so right away, thus preventing it from festering into a spreading, poisonous sore. Like the old wives say, an ounce of prevention is worth a pound of cure.

Don't keep putting off a confrontation with your problem until you really are in serious trouble. YOU HAVE A BRAIN. YOU CAN CONTROL YOUR OWN BEHAVIOUR. YOU CAN CHANGE. So *IF YOU HAVE A PROBLEM WITH YOUR DRINKING*, **DEAL WITH IT *NOW*!!!**

Chapter 7

Being Young, Foolish and 'Getting Wasted'

Like everyone else, you will experience inebriation roughly according to the blood alcohol level you reach during a drinking session. The research on the subject also suggests that, when age, weight, gender and other factors are controlled, adolescents are likely to get more intoxicated sooner than adults.

Why?

You – you adolescent or twenty something you — are likely to be more easily intoxicated than an adult because, as an adolescent, you are probably a less experienced drinker than most adults. That lack of experience means that you probably have a lower tolerance level for alcohol than most adults. It is also likely that you are still experimenting with alcohol. As part of that process, you are likely to consciously try to get intoxicated, if only for the experience. Intent is an important element in the chain of activities that lead to any type of mood-modification, whether reinforced by ingested alcohol (or other stimulants or depressants) or not.

Youth and drunkenness combine in very distressing and costly ways.

Binge drinking is widespread among youth. The United States Centers for Disease Control and Prevention (commonly referred to as "CDC") report that approximately ninety percent of the alcohol consumed by high school students is consumed in the course of binge drinking.[4] That's significantly

---

4 To secure this data, the CDC used the Behavioural Risk Factor Surveillance System and the National Youth Risk Behaviour Survey to collect data on self reports of binge drinking during the past month for 412,000 adults aged 18

higher than even adult binge drinking, amongst whom which more than half of the alcohol consumed by adults is consumed in the course of binge drinking. Among drinkers, one-third of adults and two-thirds of high school kids binge drink.

"If excessive alcohol consumption every day is problem drinking, what is the occasional stint of up to five drinks at one sitting? The answer for many might be 'a party,' and "that's just what makes binge drinking so dangerous," according to Dr. David L. Katz, director of the Prevention Research Center at Yale University School of Medicine.

"While it resides in the realm of social acceptability, it is, in fact, a major cause of alcohol-related death, and the major cause of such deaths among adolescents and young adults. No party is worth the cost of a young life, full of promise," Katz added.

In assessing the costs of drunken behaviour among minors in the United States researchers D.T. Levy, T.R. Miller and K.C. Cox (1999) estimated that for every .35c profit for a can of beer sold to a minor in the United States, there were $1.15 billion incurred in the "social harm costs." Those costs included such diverse outcomes as work loss costs, legal costs, medical and insurance costs for overdoses, accidents, assaults, and acts of rape.

In another study, estimates of multi-problem adolescent behaviour in the United States, the computations of Miller (2004) indicated that, in 1998, the multiple medical and social costs of binge drinking over the life times of youth aged under 21 years at the time of the study would amounted to $42 billion in dollars at par with their valuation in 1998.

Early Drinking: Short and Long-term Consequences

Those countries in which drinking is accepted, even for young children, as a beverage that is a normal part of meals and social life from an early age tend to have fewer problems with alcohol dependency. As I have

---

and older and over 16,000 high school students. For more information on binge drinking, visit the U.S. Centers for Disease Control and Prevention (Copyright © 2010 . Healthday)

previously noted, many experts believe that by taking alcohol off the "cultural taboo list" for children and young teens, the allure of secretive, heavy and therefore dangerous drinking is diminished. The cross-national data seems to support this view. A pattern of regular, early drinking, in amounts greater than a small glass or two of wine per meal or social event, does carry significant risks along with it, however. This is especially true in North America, where drinking at an early age is considered extremely inappropriate, with or without the accompaniment of parents.

> **Adolescents develop a tolerance for alcohol faster than adults. This places them at higher risk than adults for drinking too much because they quickly learn that they are able to consume a great deal. However, by drinking so much, they are also much more likely to, quite literally, drink themselves to death.**

A report from the National Institute of Alcohol Abuse and Alcoholism (NIAAA) suggests that, in North America, underage drinking is indeed a serious problem that can jeopardize an individual's health and various lifetime prospects. The NIAAA report indicates that the younger the age that a person begins to drink on a frequent basis, the greater the probability that an individual will at some point in their life develop an alcohol disorder. The study provides data showing that, compared with those individuals who didn't start drinking until they were 21 years old, children who started drinking before the age of 15 were four times more likely to become alcohol dependents.

Here are some facts worth knowing about early stinkin' drinkin':

- Teens that begin drinking *before* age 15 are 5 times more likely to develop an addiction to alcohol than those who begin drinking at age 21.

- An early age of drinking as a frequent practice is associated with alcohol-related episodes involving violence. What that means is that much of the violence associated with adolescence occurs as part of a drinking episode.

- Binge drinking begins for many North American youth around 13 years of age and increases throughout adolescence. It peaks in the 18-22 year old age cohort and then gradually declines as people mature in age.

- Some estimates indicate that there are over 3 million American teenagers who are alcoholics (i.e., they are clinically alcohol-dependent). Several more million can be diagnosed as problem drinkers and many more millions occasionally engage in episodes of drunken behaviour that place themselves and others at significant safety risks.

Comparisons Between Youth and Adults

Under the influence of alcohol, youth, compared with adults, are especially prone to automobile accidents and automobile fatalities that implicate self and others (*Note*: The research suggests that alcohol-impaired teenagers give into peer pressure a lot easier than those who haven't been drinking). Other forms of accident and injury are also elevated substantially when drinking is implicated. The relationship between injury, death and driving and drinking is particularly strong among young people. Consider the following:

- Each year in the United States, approximately 5,000 young people under the age of 21 years old die from causes associated with alcohol use (the National Institutes of Health, 2006). This includes deaths from motor vehicle accidents, as well as 1,600 homicides and 300 suicides. In fact, the three leading causes of death for 15 to 24 years olds are automobile accidents, suicides and homicides—and alcohol is a significant factor in all three.

- Each year, drinking among college students contributes to an estimated 1,700 student deaths and 600,000 injuries (Note: When drinking, adolescents are far more likely to commit self-injury, such as "cutting," and suicides), as well as 700,000 assaults, 90,000 sexual assaults and 474,000 cases of unprotected sex.

- Hundreds of teenagers in North America are injured or die from falls, drowning and burns in circumstances in which alcohol is implicated.

- Frequent binge drinking and alcohol dependency are also associated with several mental health problems, such as depression, anxiety, and what psychiatrists call oppositional defiant disorder (ODD)[5] and anti-social personality disorder[6] (both terms being used to refer to troubled kids who not only don't play by the rules but preoccupy themselves with a persistent and destructive defiance of them

- It is also the case that people who are drinking tend to do a lot of things that they normally wouldn't do when not under the influence of alcohol. As an example, practicing safe sex is far less likely to occur when teens have been drinking heavily.

Other heightened, injurious probabilities for teens when under the influence of alcohol include:

- emotionally scarring verbal assaults and humiliating/shaming behaviour

- physical fighting that all too often leads to serious injury or even death and serious emotional, social and legal repercussions (including criminal prosecutions, incarceration or probation)

- misadventures that lead to vandalism, break and enter and theft, which often lead to criminal prosecutions and jail time

- job loss for those who are employed (whether part-time before finishing school or full-time, upon completion)

---

5 As the term would suggest, Oppositional Defiant Disorder is a clinical mental health disorder of childhood and adolescence in which the individual exhibits a pattern of negative, defiant and hostile behaviour for a period of at least 6 months. During the time, the individual is touchy, especially sensitive, defiant and hostile, and s/he may often lose his/her temper, is persistently argumentative and disobedient with adults, tends to be angry and resentful and may deliberately and actively annoy others.

6 Anti-social personality disorder is a chronic pattern. of disregard for and violation of the rights of others. often beginning as early as age 15 years but typically setting in after 18 years old. Impulsive behaviour is common to those with this disorder. The individual is nonconforming, deceitful, irresponsible, tends to disregard social obligations and debt, is soften irritable and aggressive, and tends to lack remorse for transgressions against others.

- a significantly diminished quality of relationships with parents, siblings, friends and intimates
- participating in unprotected sex that results in sexually transmitted diseases and unplanned pregnancies that are devastating for the lifestyle and opportunities both for the baby and the mother
- pregnancies that result in newborns with Fetal Alcohol Spectrum Disorder (FASD), a life-long condition.

Stinkin' Drinkin' and the Teen Brain

Drinking on a regular basis or even to great excess on occasion during adolescence may significantly impair the basic brain functions of memory and learning. In fact, studies of experimental mice and rats has shown that, compared with adult heavy drinkers, high levels of alcohol use during adolescence is associated with more extensive damage in certain regions of the brain.

Children and adolescents can often learn with greater ease than adults. This appears to be the case with the learning of a foreign language, mastering a sport, playing a musical instrument or learning and using a computer. This enhanced capacity is primarily due to the great adaptability of the brain during one's early years.

Research has shown that the brain is not physiologically mature until a person's mid-twenties. Maturation of the brain does not occur at the same pace in the different organs which, taken together, comprise what we consider the entire brain. Most important amongst these differences is the gap in the speed of maturation between those parts of the brain that stimulate emotion and motivation (the limbic system) and the parts that involve reasoning and judgement (the prefrontal cortex), the latter of which functions to temper or regulate emotional expression and motivation. In short, those functions which serve to self-regulate, plan and reason do not keep up with the limbic system; they do not become sufficiently mature to exert control over the impulsive and emotional reactions that the limbic system generates. Thus, if heavy alcohol use occurs with great frequency, the damage it causes to the adolescent brain may limit the growth of the teenager's capacity for mature decision-making and moral reasoning. During human adolescence, the frontal regions of the brain are substantially remoulded and rewired as teenagers learn to acquire adult decision-making skills, such as the ability to focus, to discriminate, to predict and to consider questions of right and wrong.

To rephrase and summarize the point, frequent, heavy alcohol consumption creates disruption in the parts of the brain essential for self-control, motivation and goal-setting and it can compound pre-existing psychological and genetic abnormalities. Amongst other problems associated with this gap between emotional maturation and rational self-control, is the fact that early, heavy drinking may cause damage that encourages long-term alcohol dependency.

As I've noted above, recent research suggests that adolescent alcohol consumption may affect cognitive functioning and or change the developing brain in ways that increase the risk of future dependence. Studies using animal models (rodents) have indicated that alcohol has a greater adverse impact on learning and memory-related brain functions in adolescents compared with adults. At least one study of humans has also shown that a single, moderate dose of alcohol can disrupt learning more powerfully in people in their early twenties, compared with those in their late twenties.

There is now mounting research that indicates that heavy drinking during adolescence causes more damage to developing teen brains than it does to fully developed, adult brains. While there is considerable research to complete before the detail of the impact of adolescent drinking on the brain is filled in, there is now good reason to challenge the assumption that people can drink heavily for years before causing themselves significant brain injury.

The effects of repeated alcohol consumption during adolescence may also be long-lasting. Studies in humans have shown impairment of thinking for weeks after regular, heavy drinking adolescents have quit drinking altogether, as well as a different pattern of brain responses to tests of memory than among non-abusers. Other research using brain imaging techniques has shown a reduction in the size of the hippocampus in the adolescent substance abuser population. The hippocampus is a part of the brain involved in memory and activities requiring spatial navigation.

So the answer is "yes," early, frequent drinking and heavy drinking can and does cause brain damage.

Stinkin' Drinkin' and School Work

Frequent drinking binges and regular heavy drinking may be both a cause and effect of poor school performance. Studies do show that there is a negative relationship between the two. A study completed in 2000 examining an adolescent population found that, compared with non-drinkers, heavy drinkers were almost six times as likely to cut classes or skip school and binge drinkers almost five times as likely as non-drinkers to skip school or cut classes (Greenblat, 2000). The same study found that heavy drinkers were almost twice as likely as non-drinkers to exhibit poor academic performance in school as non-drinkers.

A more recent study published in the August, 2011 issue of *Alcoholism: Clinical and Experimental Research*, Spanish researcher Maria Parada and her colleagues addressed the question of whether or not binge drinking affected the memory of young adults. They examined 122 Spanish university students aged 18 to 22. Of that sample, 62 engaged in binge drinking and 60 did not. All the students were administered tests to measure their ability to learn from spoken instructions, to remember spoken instructions and visual memory capacity. The main finding was that, in healthy university students, there was a clear association between binge drinking and a diminished ability to learn new verbal information. The researchers found this explanation to hold even after factoring out other possible influences, including varying intellectual levels (i.e., measured with "I.Q." tests), history of brain disorders or psychological disorders, and other drug use, and gender.

In addition to its other findings, the Spanish study added evidence to other, previous findings, that there was diminished memory capacity in adolescents who engage in frequent, heavy drinking episodes.

Richard W. Thatcher

Pressures to be a Stinkin' Drinker

As a North American youth, there is a lot of pressure on you to engage in careless drinking activity. There are also counter-pressures. In fact, there is a regular flow of pro and con messages streamed to you. Faced with these contradictory messages, you will have to make up your own mind about whether or not heavy drinking will be part of your lifestyle.

Establishing a sensible, long-term drinking strategy is not the easiest thing to do, of course, especially given the various influences in play that encourage you to carelessly indulge in a whimsical fashion or, in other words, on the basis of mood and circumstance. So, from the thinkin' drinker's perspective, let's identify some of the influences that will weigh on your decision. After all, when you develop any kind of strategy, it's important to know what you're up against.

Let's consider some of the more powerful influences that weigh upon your drinking choices: (1) the role modeling of others (2) the influence of the media and (3) the influence of peer culture.

The Contribution of Role Modeling to Drinking Behaviour

Many of the strongest messages about drinking are not overtly communicated with specific statements. They are conveyed by way of a far more subtle but sometimes no less influential practice called "role modelling."

Role modelling refers to a process by which one person observes the behaviour of another (individual or group) and, as a result, seriously considers adopting the other's behaviour, thus making it their own. In short, modelling is essentially imitative behaviour. It involves adopting behaviour because we observe its enactment by others we admire or envy. We imitate it because we think it is stylish, admirable and worthy of imitation or simply because we think that adopting the behaviour pattern would benefit us in some way.

The fact is that much of our character and personal habits are formed through role modelling, so, of itself, the activity is neither bad nor good. In fact, it is a key part of human socialization—and socialization is the way that we build and maintain societies—and societies are the web of interpersonal relationships through which we humans survive and reproduce.

What is bad or good is the nature of what is being modeled.

The drinking messages that can be conveyed by any of the people that exert a special influence on us might be very sensible ones. Abstinence or controlled and limited drinking can be part of one's family culture. It can also be an expectation that prevails among our close friends. In fact, for most people, frequent, heavy drinking and drunken behaviour are actually frowned upon more often than not, looked upon with derision, and regarded as being wholly unacceptable.

The opposite can also be true, however. Older members of a household might regularly drink after work, maybe on Friday with co-workers or at house parties or any variety of festive occasions. Dad or mom pouring that drink before supper or having a few too many beer on a regular basis while watching a favourite television show in the living room may well be something you have grown up with.

> The drinking styles of parents and older brothers and sisters can have a great influence on us. But in the end, we are responsible for our own actions. Whatever the behaviour of dad or mom regarding alcohol – or for that matter, big brother or sister, or a really cool pal or neighborhood leader — it is not the key to your own, mature approach to drinking. The key to sensible drinking is in your own brain.

The Influence of Media and Advertising

Okay, let's turn to the media's persuasive influence. It is hardly a revelation to say that the entertainment and information media, including television, radio, movies, newspapers, magazines, and the Internet, are also major players in the game of communicating messages about drinking beverage alcohol. Again, contradictory messages about drinking are woven into the fabric of the multi-media communications systems that are a regular part of contemporary life. Cautionary, often very in-your-face, public service messages about the dangers of drinking assail you, competing directly with advertising and various forms of direct and subtly embedded messages that promote alcohol consumption, even heavy drinking.

Police departments, state and provincial alcohol regulatory agencies and voluntary organizations such as Mothers Against Drunk Driving (MADD) warn against the risks of heavy alcohol use on radio, TV, newspapers, in health education classes and on billboards. These agencies are joined by organizations, especially Alcoholics Anonymous and various church organizations in offering public warnings against heavy drinking. They also plead with alcoholics and their loved ones to seek help, often through an initial, confrontational but caring intervention.

At least partially running counter to these anti-drunkenness messages are pro-drinking messages, which are delivered both directly and indirectly by the various divisions of the alcohol manufacturing and sales industry. Advertisers and marketing agencies work on behalf of companies that either produce alcoholic beverages or that include liquor, beer or wine sales as profit units within their overall mix of sales items (think of hotels, restaurants and the tourist and entertainment industry in general, and professional and even some amateur sports).

Beverage alcohol promotions, some subtle, some blunt and forthright, attempt, all too often successfully, to persuade youth to link alcohol with positive, pleasurable outcomes, such as the enhanced enjoyment of social and recreational events. The fun of drinking while going to the races or a football game or while bowling or golfing (with beer delivered via a mobile cart by comely young ladies), or drinking while watching any game with friends in a bar or at home in a family room: these are all captured in TV ads that intended to inspire positive associations between the observation of high level sports, camaraderie and drinking. You and I know the implication in these messages that we drink at least to the point of getting a "buzz."

Let me list some examples.

- Glitzy magazines and daily television are full of clever ads promoting vodka and whiskey by showing a bunch of healthy, attractive, good-humoured young people intensely enjoying each other's company at a restaurant or Caribbean vacation spot.

- Novelty T-shirts promoting beer seem to be everywhere. Beer companies are amazingly effective at finding out where major events are being held and giving deals to event organizers for the shipment of truckloads of full beer cases. And then there's all those "tailgate" parties that offer beer and hotdogs before, during and sometimes even after race car events and football games.

- We've all seen those full page magazine ads that display amber mugs of ale in the hands of handsome and beautiful young people smiling and chatting before the glow of a fire in a cedar chalet at the end of an exciting if strenuous day of skiing at a mountain resort. Admit it, they're pretty effective ads.

- Alcohol ads do not stop at creating associations with fun and camaraderie, however. Sex is also on the associational agenda. Think of all those commercials showing a couple at a candle light dinner or a late night cocktail. Watch closely and you'll find the veiled suggestion that the drinking is the key that opens the door to later bedroom intimacies. In all of this, drinking is promoted through blatant advertising messages that link beer or wine to being part of the crowd, to prestige, even, ironically to athleticism (How many beer commercials show "all the gang" enjoying a "cool one?"), to sexual fulfilment, even to creativity and success. In all of this, there is the hidden sub-text that to be cool is to be a robust drinker.

- While Hollywood has become far more responsible in this regard, many movies and television programs still portray continuous drinking in an extremely positive light or at least in a fashion that underlines sexiness, style, and sheer enjoyment and fun. Drunkenness is also frequently portrayed in movies with affectionate humour – see the remake of *Arthur* or *Hangover* recently — or at least great sympathy. Over time, Hollywood has probably been the most effective organizational influence on the popularization of alcohol use. For decades actors typified by their glamour and popularity with audiences were shown in attractive, stylized ways on the big screen, elegantly sipping on and offering liquor to other people in grand gestures.

Then there are the comedies that build a mischievous and naughty but affectionate association between heavy drinking and school holidays. Those teen-targeted comedies about Spring break in Florida have created an entire promotional theme out of equating wild, drunken teen holidays with an intense good time, hah-hah-hah dumb-dumb humour and sexual conquest.

- There is mounting evidence that the media personalities that are most popular with young people are cultural trendsetters. When your favourite actor or professional athlete in the public eye is shown or known as a smoker, heavy drinker, heavy drug user, arrogant cad or nasty "mother#$%@*x," thousands of impressionable young people decide those habits are kind of cool. You know, the old "If it's good enough for them, then maybe I'll join the parade."

- Television has an even bigger influence on adolescent behaviour than movies, of course, partially because of the sheer amount of time spent before the TV set. These ads reach millions of teens and children. The messages in the ads appeal to the humour, sense of fantasy, and identification with sports and other glamorous and popular media stars.

Research shows that adolescent habits are significantly influenced by the behaviour of television and movie stars and admired sports figures. This I call "secondary role modelling" because it is not delivered to you through direct, ongoing contact with real people. The most popular of these celebrities can attract literally millions of other young people to habitual alcohol and tobacco use. If they are known to smoke or drink, there's a lot of impressionable teens and young adults out there who follow suit. Television and, more recently, the Internet, are the technologies that make those celebrities and their habits familiar to an incredibly wide audience.

- Skilled at blurring the lines between online advertising, information and market research, beverage alcohol companies have become quite effective in using the Internet to promote their products among teens. Major beverage companies are a major presence on the Web, appealing to teens and younger children looking for games, articles, and clothing–and many teens can't distinguish between the facts and the hype. In fact, the Center for Media Education (CME), which monitors online advertising, has found that beverage alcohol band icons are all over the Internet Web landscape.

Peer Culture

In North America, during an ordinary week in the life of an adolescent, there is more exposure to peers than to adults, including parents or any individual teacher. If you didn't know, the term "peer" refers to those who are similar to you in terms of your social circumstances. In your case, think age and broadly similar cultural similarities. The adolescent peer group exerts an enormous social influence on youth.

Much of the influence of the adolescent peer group has to do with the fact that not only during the hours spent at school but after school, and well into the early 20s, youth are with far more adolescents than they are with adults. In their middle school and high school years, even most of the individual teachers North American adolescents see are only in their presence for one or two classes per day–and this type of limited exposure extends into community colleges, technical institutes, colleges and universities.

> **For most of the day, American and Canadian adolescents have little contact with their parents and they tend to be primarily influenced by their peers. When they first go out to work or enter post-secondary schooling, the direct influence of parents is pushed right off their radar screens.**

For most of the day, the majority of North American adolescents have little contact with their parents, often not even their siblings, if they have any. Why? Because parents are typically working outside the home and social interaction is age-segregated, which means that you tend to hang out with kids who are close to your own age and, most often, in the same grade.

The sisters or brothers that you may have are likely to follow the same pattern, so that even if you tried to have a more family-oriented social life, it might not be possible. In addition, after-school and weekend activities take young people outside the home or into gaming alongside friends or "virtual" friends in a mini-world with which most adults have little acquaintance.

When young people graduate to the workplace after high school or move into technical training, college or university studies, parents often become almost completely removed from their daily lives.

Youth culture is not cut of one cloth of course. As a segment of society, adolescents and young adults have come to generate a variety of distinctive, full-blown sub-cultures that divide them by values, preferred recreational activities, taste in music and dance, movie and television preferences, clothes, hair styles, and even skin decorations (e.g., tattoos, piercings, etc.). These divisions are reinforced by a clever, multi-billion dollar advertising, image-making and product marketing industry that views youth as an extremely significant consumer group. There is money, big money, in d'em d'ere youthful hills, and there's a lot of cunning business people who are specialists in mining it out.

Conclusion

The many and frequent messages communicated to you on a regular basis by individuals and groups of various persuasions and motives regarding problem drinking are mixed and contradictory and, for this reason, they can be very confusing. There are probably more messages prompting you to at least experiment with heavy drinking. Whatever the final balance of influence in these messages, only YOU can sort the wheat from the chaff in deciding what makes sense. Only you can make the decisions about drinking that involve your own personal behaviour. This book was written to help you do just that.

Chapter 8

Risk Factors for Becoming an Alcoholic

Fortunately, most of you are not currently and will never be alcoholics. The problem is not rare, however and, as a population, you are exposed to various degrees of risk that you will acquire the problem.

As I have noted above, some estimates suggest that approximately 3 million adolescents in the United States can be clinically described as "alcohol dependents" (in common terminology, "alcoholics"). I'm very suspicious about the accuracy of those numbers, however, because the term alcohol dependency is itself used far too liberally, even by addiction researchers—and *alcoholic* is commonly used without reference to any specific definition.

Even if substantially exaggerated, the very size of such estimates is scary. They do strongly support the view that alcohol problems, including alcohol dependency, among your peers, should be treated by policy-makers as a major public health problem.

One of the most significant risks of frequent, heavy drinking, is habit formation, the intensification and reinforcement of that habit and then, yes, unadulterated addiction to alcohol. If you come to routinely rely on any mood-altering substance, including alcohol, whether to enhance your social life, to cope with the unpleasant aspects of your life, or to relieve yourself of a painful mental state such as anxiety, depression or anger, you are establishing an intense habit that can become increasingly hard to break.

An intense drinking habit can establish not only psychological dependence on alcohol but physical dependence. The former refers to an individual's conscious or semi-conscious attitude that alcohol is needed for the achievement of a sense of psychological and emotional comfort.

Physical dependence refers to feelings of physical discomfort and cravings in the absence of the alcohol, as well as a pattern of increasing biological tolerance.

By "tolerance" I mean that your body (i.e., your 'physiology'), including your brain, gradually adapts to (i.e., it becomes increasingly able to 'tolerate') more and more quantities of a mood-modifying substance, which is in this case, alcohol. What that means is that the pleasurable high you get when you initially become a frequent drinker diminishes over time and that high requires gradually increased doses of the substance. The alcohol gradually becomes the central preoccupation in your life as you continually seek to satisfy your need for it. That need is so great that other, very important, practical aspects of your life become secondary to your craving. In short, your increasing habit has transformed you into an addict.

Alcohol Problems as Addictions

In simple terms, an addiction is a comforting, sometimes relieving, or pleasurable habit that we find very, very difficult to wilfully change, despite the fact that, while it gives us short-term pleasure, it yields very damaging long-term consequences.

An addiction creates a variety of personal problems, including diminished physical and mental health and an undermining of your basic moral foundation.

When I refer to the term "moral" I'm not getting high and mighty. I'm talking about the foundation of basic values and principles that you have learned to live by. The burden of guilt associated with dumb drinking behaviour compromises your basic ethical standards and, in an effort to relieve yourself of that burden, you begin to adjust your sense of morality downward. Your moral bottom line is therefore lowered to accommodate the addiction and reduce the guilt—and that lowering can continue until your basic moral foundation crumbles. Dependency on alcohol can become more intense over time and thus it becomes increasingly hard to overcome.

If you hadn't thought about it, it might be of interest to you to consider the fact that the root word of the term *intoxication* is "toxic," which means "poison." It doesn't take a rocket scientist to figure out that regularly drinking heavy doses of a poisonous substance is tantamount to suicide in slow motion. If you were to speed up the process by driving your blood alcohol level up through the rafters, the resulting alcohol poisoning would kill you very quickly.

In short, alcohol dependency – or "alcoholism" – is essentially a drug addiction, with alcohol being the drug.

Alcohol Mis-use and Other Drugs

People who become addicted to alcohol are also frequently attracted to other drugs; especially drugs that help them cope with psychological or social factors that cause them severe emotional pain. For this reason, alcohol is sometimes referred to as a "gateway drug." In other words, once you've tried one, what the heck, you might as well try another. The guilt belt has snapped off anyway. You go in the front gate and you can quickly move through the door and various gates in the backyard, in each of which there is another mood-modifying drug to get hooked on. It's a depression prospect.

That gateway process amplifies the problems of alcohol for those who move on to other drugs. Mixing mood-modifying drugs of any kind can have severely negative effects on your state of health.

Many alcohol addicts stick to alcohol alone, however, leaving additional drugs to others. There are some notable exceptions, of course. Tobacco, especially in the form of cigarettes, coffee (and other caffeinated beverages) and most "junk foods," are common friends of the alcohol-dependent. While these have very limited mind-altering consequences, they do almost immediately provide a certain amount of physical or psychic comfort. Unfortunately, the combined addictions of tobacco and drinking can make the challenge of overcoming either even more difficult and, of course, there is a truckload of health problems and personal consequences that follow.

The Factors that Enable Alcohol Problems Vary Widely

Typically, the onset of an addiction is recognized both by the individual with the problem and those around him (or her). The person who is becoming alcohol dependent often resists that emerging knowledge, however, initially developing a state of denial as he or she begins to fear that something very unhealthy, even dangerous, is happening to them.

It is also the case that many, perhaps most people with an emerging drinking problem, tend to know that their drinking is getting out of hand and they are truly concerned about the negative consequences associated with their drinking habit. Yet despite this realization, a high risk drinking habit has often become woven into a complex set of ordinary behaviour patterns, like perking up in the morning, having a cigarette, relaxing after school, and socializing on the weekend. These linked activities become a source of compelling motivation unto themselves. The individual therefore finds that it is very, very hard just to quit or to reduce to safer levels the frequency of drinking sessions or the amount drunk in individual sessions.

I've indicated that early onset drinking – that is, frequent drinking at an early, pre-adult age – is a risk factor for the acquisition of alcohol dependency on the arrival of adulthood. There are also circumstances and individual characteristics that appear to make some people especially vulnerable to acquiring a destructive dependency on alcohol. Let's consider the factors that scientific investigation has indicated have an increased probability of fostering alcohol dependency.

Genetics is a Key Predisposing Factor

There is now a consensus in the medical and behavioural science literature that there is indeed an appropriately described medical (psychiatric) disorder called "alcohol dependency," which is now referred to as a "psychiatric disorder." The research also strongly indicates that a genetic predisposition (one's biological inheritance) is one of the most significant factors in determining who will and who will not acquire this condition after consuming beverage alcohol over several sessions.

Thinkin' Drinkin'

The relevant research on alcoholics (i.e., alcohol dependents) who enter treatment in North America indicates that 80% to 85% have a parent or grandparent with a history of alcoholism (alcohol dependency). Such survey research does not prove that genetics cause the alcohol dependency syndrome, however. After all, the syndrome could very well be *learned* in alcoholic families, more a problem of imitation than any pre-determined biological programming.

The idea that genetics trumps learning for some is supported by human *adoption studies*, however. These studies compare human twins, one of whom has been separated at an early age from his or her alcoholic parent(s)' home. The evidence in these studies has been consistent. Even when raised in homes with non-alcoholic parents, sons and daughters of alcohol-dependents are more likely to become alcoholics than people born to parents with no history of alcoholism. The best estimates suggest there is a 3-fold increase in the likelihood of alcoholism among those with alcoholic parents, even if only one of the members of the study group's parents was alcoholic.

The research also suggests that not only is alcohol dependency influenced by a genetic predisposition but also by the transformation of one's brain chemistry as a result of lengthy and recurring bouts of drinking.

It is also the case that alcohol dependency can and does result from socialization and mere practise. Culture, including law and religion, obviously enter the picture. Some societies are far less tolerant than others of widespread alcohol use and access to the beverage itself is very difficult in some. So when the harsh judgement of others, penalties and lack of opportunity are roadblocks, then alcohol dependency rates in a society are very low. When attitudes are far more relaxed and access is easy, then the prospect of widespread alcohol dependency increases substantially.

Genetics and Types of Alcohol-Dependents

Not all addicted drinkers are cut of the same cloth. In the late 1980s, studies of Swedish adoptees by Robert C. Cloninger indicated there may actually be two common, different types of alcoholic (see Cloninger, 1983).

Cloninger's data described what he referred to as a Type 1 alcoholic, who may be either female or male, and who develops a problem with alcohol beyond their teens, in their adult years. According to Cloninger's investigations, the Type 1 alcoholic can abstain and is rarely involved in petty criminality, with the significant exception of driving while impaired. This group shows major problems with the loss of control when they drink.

The second alcoholic Cloninger describes is the Type 2 alcoholic; male, tends to show problems with alcohol in his early teens, has great difficulty abstaining from alcohol, and expresses a lifestyle characterized by anti-social behaviour and petty crime.

Both environment and genetics tends to play a role in Type 1 alcoholism; however, Type 2 alcoholism may need only a combination of exposure to drinking and genetics to move the affected individual to a pattern of alcoholism.

Thus, genetic research on humans has shown that genetics often plays a role in the acquisition of alcoholic behaviour. However, no single gene (i.e., an "alcogene") has been shown to cause alcoholism and the evidence suggests that several genes may be involved.

Other studies focusing on inherited brain chemistry have lent significant support to the idea that genetics can play a key role in producing some forms of alcohol dependency.

Non-Genetic Drivers of Alcohol Problems

It is important to recognize that genetic predisposition to alcohol dependence or problem drinking does not necessarily lead to alcohol dependence. Unlike an infection, an addiction is not entirely forced on an individual. In fact, the victim must go through a number of steps to become addicted, including all the work and money required to secure the substance on a regular basis and all the social relations that must be reshaped because of the eccentric behaviours associated directly with the drinking. As Harold Doweiko, a writer of a well-known text on substance abuse, has noted, with irony, "If it took as much time and energy to 'catch' a cold, pneumonia, or cancer, it is doubtful that 'any' of us would ever be sick a day in our lives!"

As with most behaviour, individuals do make choices regarding how they manage the influence of their predisposition. For example, many males can be said to possess a genetic mix that encourages physical aggression in the settling of disputes. That may include personality factors such as a combative mind set, impatience and great, natural physical strength, thick bones, large hands and excellent athletic ability, and a thick jaw and facial bone structure. Yet, depending on the socialization of that individual and the choices s/he makes, that predisposition may be a dominant personality and behavioural trait exhibited in either socially acceptable or wholly unacceptable ways. In some instances, social influences to which the individual is subjected in their early years may completely repress or may never be exhibited. All of us have met the strong, extremely athletic individual who could easily defeat almost anyone in our high school but is an entirely gentle, respectful and unaggressive individual, except on the basketball court, ball diamond or football field.

Just like the choices we have in managing a predisposition to aggression, the choices that establish alcohol consumption patterns are influenced by social learning and they are also reinforced by either one or a combination of psychological and social factors. In part, this reasoning is supported by the fact that, in the absence of social learning, human beings are unable to acquire even the most basic behaviours required for basic survival. Even the higher primates are utterly dependent on social learning to acquire such basic functions as procreative sex and mother/infant bonding.

Finally, we must never forget that most fully human quality of our behaviour is free will. We must remember that alcohol problems are a behaviour; they are not, of themselves, a *disease*, even if they are a "predisposition" (basically, a statistical correlation that finds a recurrent pattern in several generations of a family). I say this because, unlike other problems referred to as "diseases," alcohol abuse and other drug addictions require the active participation of the victim and the physical act of consumption itself. Cancer or tuberculosis do not require such choices.

The Bio-psycho-social Model for Explaining Alcohol Addiction (Alcoholism)

The most sophisticated thinking about the causes and behavioural correlates of problem drinking take all these factors into account as possible influences on acquired alcohol dependency. There now appears to be a broad consensus that, while one or more factors may weigh heavily as causes of alcoholic outcomes, complex interactions between various biological, psychological and social factors can contribute to the development of addiction problems. Not surprisingly, research scientists in the addictions field call the most valid current understanding of alcohol problems the *bio-psycho-social* model of explanation. Scientists who adhere to this model argue that the question regarding what causes alcoholism is not a question of nature versus nurture but rather to what degree and in what manner various possible influencing factors contribute to a problem drinking outcome.

This updated model assumes is that, while some people may have an inherited predisposition to certain kinds of alcohol problems, there are many psychological and social factors that may also contribute. In addition, it must be recognized that active, voluntary choices made by the individual are necessary before any alcohol problem becomes manifest.

The rather wide range of factors that might contribute to problem drinking and alcohol dependency, are outlined below.

- *Mood*: It seems obvious and it's true: the mood you are in prior to drinking and that you develop during a drinking session can have a strong influence on the outcomes of the experience, including the amount that you drink. The mood that a drinker brings to the process of use also has an influence on his or her tolerance level and behaviour during and immediately after heavy drinking.

- *Disordered, self-defeating thought patterns*, such as low self-esteem and low perceptions of self-competence, can reduce an individual's willingness or ability to resist peer pressure to drink or take drugs.

- *Expectations based on what one has heard from others*: Both adolescents and adults who drink will have their alcohol experience shaped not only by the alcohol itself but also by their expectations of what the alcohol will do. Placebo experiments have shown that a user's expectations about the effects of alcohol can have a strong influence on its on the behaviour of the individual during and after a drinking episode, whether or not they have actually drank alcoholic beverages or not (so long as they believe they have). A drinker's expectations can be derived from many sources, including watching parents or older siblings, a friend's accounts, education, the mass media, or descriptions by health educators.

- *Anticipations of drinking outcomes from past experience with alcohol*: Familiarity with the experience of using alcohol is an important determinant of a drug's effects. Initially, the experimental use of alcohol often produces an immediate and excessive "drunk," whereas the same amount, taken after many bouts of "learning" to drink, is likely to have a milder intoxicating influence. At least in part, tolerance for alcohol is a learned response.

- *Modelling*: As I've noted above, through behavioural modelling and other forms of *social learning* and reinforcement, human beings learn drinking comportment. This means that what goes on during a drinking episode is largely a learned set of behaviours. An individual can learn civil and co-operative drinking behaviour (thinkin' drinkin') or "acting up" (stinkin' drinkin') behaviour, depending on the most influential messages received about drinking in one's past. Parental behaviour is the biggest single influence on the long-term behaviour of children.

- *Social attachment*: People in close and satisfying terms with intimate partners and families of origin are less likely to have serious alcohol problems than those who are socially isolated or lacking in family connections, friendships or intimate contacts.

- *An unstable home environment*: Angry reactions to neglectful or abusive parents may also result in alcohol problems for the affected children. Many observers have argued that the most likely causes of problem drinking lie in the effects of family instability. If that instability has characterized your early life, then it is important to figure out ways to avoid self-destructive tendencies that have grown out of your home—and to ensure that you do not simply repeat the negative patterns to which you have been exposed.

- *Peer group influence*: As noted in the preceding chapter, the very direct influence of one's peer group generally contributes significantly to an individual's choice to abuse alcohol or other drugs. This is particularly true for adolescents. People often model themselves after their peers or the leadership amongst their peers. This modelling will often involve the development of both attitudes and behaviour that mimic the model.

- *Social Location*: Where one drinks matters. The reputation of a drinking venue can either constrain or facilitate various behaviours undertaken while people are under the influence of alcohol. Drinking wine at communion is likely to have a very different outcome than drinking in a tough bar.

- *The impact of nationality and culture*: Different nations have different drinking norms and their inhabitants are influenced by them. In North America, instead of introducing alcohol "normally" to children, beverage alcohol consumption is prohibited legally and it is limited legally to private residences and licensed premises for public use. Thus, it is not surprising that many young people feel that drinking alcohol is a significant activity that marks the transition to adulthood. As I have noted elsewhere in this book, in France and Italy, drinking is a normal part of growing up and there are few restrictions. Some ethnic groups, such as Native Americans and the Irish within the United States have a high proportion of problem drinkers while peoples of Chinese ethnicity have few.

- *Anxiety around sexual identity*: Excessive drinking is an especially dangerous practice for adolescents and young adults who are confused by the alternative sexual identity and sexual practice options they are exploring. Individuals from very conservative families, schools, friendship networks and communities often go through feelings of self-loathing as they observe or experience the lack of flexibility in the world around them. If an alternative gender orientation is an emerging preference, a wall of stigma and bullying often poses an overwhelming wall of resistance. As a means of venting or dealing with these anxieties, excessive drinking can lead to careless behaviour, self-destructive or anti-social thinking and even suicidal behaviour.

Conclusion

What you really have to know about all of this can be summarized as follows:

- ✓ IF YOUR FATHER OR MOTHER OR GRANDPARENTS WERE ALCOHOLICS, THEN YOU MAY WELL BE GENETICALLY PREDISPOSED TO THE PROBLEM AND YOU PROBABLY SHOULDN'T DRINK. IF YOU DO, YOU *MUST* DO IT IN A VERY PLANNED AND CONTROLLED WAY!

- ✓ IN ADDITION TO GENETICS, THERE ARE MANY PSYCHOLOGICAL AND SOCIAL FACTORS WHICH, ON THEIR OWN OR ACTING TOGETHER, CAN ENABLE ALCOHOL DEPENDENCY.

- ✓ EVEN IF ALCOHOL DEPENDENCY IS NOT IN YOUR IMMEDIATE ANCESTRY BUT YOU ARE EXPOSED TO SEVERAL FACTORS THAT TEND TO STRONGLY INFLUENCE ALCOHOLIC OUTCOMES, THEN YOU MUST ACTIVELY RESIST THOSE INFLUENCES OR YOU MAY BE ON YOUR ROAD TO ALCOHOL DEPENDENCY.

- ✓ THROUGH A LIFESTYLE OF FREQUENT DRINKING, ALCOHOL DEPENDENCY CAN BE ACQUIRED, SIMILAR TO THE ADDICTION THAT CAN OCCUR WITH

REGULAR USE OF ANY OTHER MOOD-MODIFYING SUBSTANCE.

It is wise to THINK about your drinking, which is the primary theme of this book.

Chapter 9

'Freeze-framing,' then Changing, Automatic Thoughts (The Foundation of the *Thinkin' Drinkin'* Strategy)

For some of you, the challenge of confronting serious alcohol problems, especially alcohol-dependency, will seem overwhelming. For you, seeking professional help and the help of supportive friends and self-help groups is essential.

The facts suggest, however, that for most of you, however, moderate (thinkin') drinking is a choice that you can and should make. You can modify stinkin' drinking behaviour, eliminate it, and find alternative behaviour as satisfying substitutes to meet the same needs.

Whether dealing with alcohol dependency, bizarre drinking patterns, or just the potential for a high risk binge, the primary tools for developing effective drinking management are the same. It is those tools that help you address the contradictory nature of habits and the automatic thinking that accompanies them.

The Importance of Habits–Benefits and Dangers

A habit can be simply defined as an acquired, repetitive behaviour pattern. Habit selection is what thinkin' drinkin' is all about.

With many other higher animal forms, human beings share the need to learn behaviour that can and will form into habits. In order to survive in a complex world, we need to develop habits. Why? Because if you had to stop and think through every situation that you face you wouldn't survive and during the time that you stayed alive, life would be an immensely slow, unproductive, and enormously risky experience. (*Note*: Consider living in the jungle and having to cope with predatory lions. Along with your peers, you'd want to have acquired some preventive and attack-specific, self-defence responses from your tribe – er . . . not just running to beat hell when the king (or queen) of the jungle has you up close in its sights — or, well . . . you'd be a goner).

Habits uniquely perform all the functions of what other animals rely upon to survive and prosper; namely genetically programmed, instinctive responses to situations. Other higher animals do learn habits; however, for human beings, our basic survival and well-being tools must be learned because they are not instinct-based (i.e., genetically programmed).

> **Habits are necessary to human functioning but there are *good* habits and there are *bad* habits; and there are some habits that are dually charged: they offer positive rewards in the short run but lead to very negative outcomes in the long run. I want you to figure out how to make drinking a good habit and, if you can't, to get rid of the habit altogether.**

So the learning of habits through informal socialization and formal education and training is fundamental to basic human survival, personal development, social development and well-being in general.

Conscious thinking, active memories, communication skills, and habit-forming processes have replaced our instincts as our basic mode of operation and survival. We depend on these capacities for dealing much that occurs in our lives. Neuroscience is gradually learning a great deal about our predispositions to form certain habits but, as far as we know today, those habits require learning to become embedded in the routines of our ongoing behaviour.

When you cross a street and a car comes lurching at you, by habit, you vamoose: you quickly get out of the way of the oncoming vehicle. If you were to stand there and contemplate your choices for even a few seconds, you wouldn't be reading this book. In fact, you probably wouldn't be a sentient being at all.

You owe those early survival habits to those who taught you how to handle traffic as a pedestrian, including what to avoid, timing and various other things when you cross a street. Thanks be to mom and dad or foster parents, older sister and/or brother and the school teachers and traffic cops who visited your school to discuss safety with you in daycare, kindergarten and early elementary school.

So the capacity to form habits through learning is a wonderful and necessary thing. But not all habits are themselves so wonderful. There are good habits, sort of good habits, not very good habits and terrible, really awful habits. Thankfully, we can change those of our habits that aren't very productive or are downright destructive.

The Half-choices that Guide Much of Our Lives

Most of your life, much of what you're thinking and doing is influenced by habit. Those habits in turn are often guided by societal norms, family rules, school dictums, and the customs of our peer groups. Yet you have also formed distinctive, personal habits and you have and will acquire such habits over a life time, some of them changing and being replaced by others as the need arises. Habit, like culture itself, is a practical thing: as evolutionary theorists will argue, human beings select those attitudes and behaviour patterns that seem to work best in a given set of circumstances and reject those that seem less effective.

The very nature of a habit is that we come to enact them almost automatically. We spontaneously initiate them when circumstances appear that repeat past situations in which our behaviour responded, more or less effectively. As a result of the very frequency of these automatic responses to specific situations, we don't have to think much about what to do in various, repetitive circumstances. So, in effect, the instructions become seeded in our subconscious, emerging when called upon.

So for much of your life, after your basic socialization has occurred, you respond more or less automatically – or at least semi-automatically — to situations on the basis of a vast repertoire of sub-conscious guidelines (norms and habits). In truth, in each instance, for an instant at least, you might question these guidelines but, for the most part, we simply follow them. Only when there is something we can observe that undermines our confidence in the effectiveness of the behaviour do we try something different, or when there is great social pressure to alter our behaviour.

In saying that you and, in fact, all of us human beings, for the most part live according to half-choices or partial choices, we are saying that, to a large extent, programmed by habits.

As you live through your teenage and young adult years, through your own efforts and the teaching and training of our others, you will build upon your early socialization and acquire a very large toolkit of habits and most of them will stay with us throughout our lives. If we really tried to change them all we would literally, go crazy. Like the philosophers in the hilarious Monty Python soccer game, we would walk about constantly thinking intensely and debating privately while the game itself never really gets underway. The players are simply too preoccupied with philosophical questions that arise with every potential move.

> **If you don't choose the norms and values that guide you and examine and select those habits that support them, then other people, circumstances and lazy predictability will do it for you.**

Habits are learned with varying degrees of intensity and they can be extinguished. A lot of our habits disappear because the circumstances that trigger their use fade and disappear over time.

Habits can also disappear if alternative behaviour is more strongly reinforced (rewarded) than an original habit. As I've said, YOU HAVE THE POWER TO ESTABLISH NEW HABITS AND TO ELIMINATE

OLD ONES! And part of maturing is becoming responsible for this very process.

Changing Bad Drinking Habits

Think about it! What does this capacity to intervene in bad habits have for drinking behaviour? Or for any other behaviour that will predictably yield immediate satisfaction but eventual pain?

The almost obvious answer is that we can bring our drinking practices into a rational balance by avoiding the circumstances that call out the dually charged habit and by substituting that habit with a singly charged, positive one.

Our 'Inner Dialogue': The Conversation Between Different Voices in Our Heads

There is now something of a consensus that human thinking in relation to guiding behaviour works through a sort of inner dialogue. This inner dialogue was central to the thinking of such famous thinkers as social-psychologist George Herbert Mead and Sigmund Freud, the father of psychoanalysis, as well as the idea of "self-talk" that is so common to contemporary, cognitive-behavioural psychologists. The concept is now sufficiently received as common wisdom that pop psychologists are forever coming up with new references to part of an interior dialogue that is part of the way we function. You've all heard the term, the "inner child."

The idea of this "inner dialogue" that we are all supposed to carry on refers to the inner conversations that we human beings engage in between a part of our mind that would like us to act on impulse in terms of our immediate feelings and at least two other voices.

One of those "other voices" is one that demands that we think in terms of principles, of whether or not the consequences of our actions will be aligned with what we believe to be right or wrong.

The other voice speaks with a concern about the longer term consequences of an action on our own well-being, for example its social impact, such as what others may think of us or the trouble we might get into if we do something. In short, we are always considering actions in terms of a debate between our immediate impulses, our ethical self (or conscience) and our consideration of its longer term consequences for us and, sometimes, those for whom we care most deeply. Between these voices competing for our favour we have the capacity to stand back, assess the different choices and then arrive at a conclusion.

Much of our habitual behaviour, perhaps most, originates in the direct or indirect influence and teaching of others. But such influences often conflict, and these circumstances provide opportunities to question and make more positive choices about our own behaviour. For example, we are conflicted when our friends all encourage heavy drinking and our parents and admired peers discourage heavy drinking. These conflicted messages alert us to the fact that we must make a choice. We can choose our behaviour. We can create new habits.

Intervening in Your Automatic Thoughts: Developing a Mediating Voice to Guide Your Drinking

Like a lot of other behaviour patterns that comprise your lifestyle, your drinking style can consist of a set of good habits, some not so good habits and some terrible habits. Whatever the actual weight given to habits as influences on our behaviour, much of what we do and even think, as human beings, is driven by habit. That means that much of what we do occurs almost spontaneously, with little or new fresh (revised) thinking. We do many, many things as a "force of habit," as they say. For all intents and purposes, what we think and what we do occurs *automatically*, our actions being dictated by a sort of sub-conscious script. Even our tendency to follow others can become and often is a habit.

As I've suggested above, most people who experience alcohol problems in their early lives (teenage and young adult years), will learn to modify those habits on their own. They will "mature out" of their bad drinking habits as they get older and as they assume greater responsibility and authority in their lives. A drinking habit can grow into an addiction, however, acquiring both a psychological and physical dependency on the substance, so it is important to nip it in the bud.

Choosing Good Drinking Habits: A Personal Initiative

If you want to truly be in charge of your drinking behaviour, rather than letting semi-conscious thoughts dictate that behaviour, you should try to determine the type of drinking that you regard as a set of desirable habits to support your efforts enjoy yourself in this way—and the habits you want to avoid. Otherwise, you will find yourself simply making your drinking choices based on generalized impulses rooted in past social influences, or maybe immediate moods such as anger, loneliness, or sadness, or even a narrowly defined, unchangeable conscience that you have left unexamined for a long, long time.

I want you to think carefully about your capacity to create good habits and to steer clear of bad ones. It is a strategy and set of skills that can make your approach to drinking a sensible one–and which can help you avoid all kinds of crazy, stupid, dumb, dangerous, regrettable stuff that can and likely will happen to you, at least in varying degrees.

The thinkin' drinkin' strategy that I propose is all about creating and sustaining good habits regarding the use of beverage alcohol.

Automatic Thoughts about Drinking

Automatic thoughts are those thoughts that we are hardly aware of but which instantaneously come prior to and motivate most of our actions. We act on them despite the fact that any obviously conscious thought has taken place. The thought that does take place is mostly a recognition scanning process that instructs us how to react to a set of memorized guidelines and external cues.

Behind our automatic thoughts are a set of assumptions and core beliefs. The thinking and action process follows the sequence on the next page.

Temptation to Drink (Who, what [and how much].
Why, when, with whom and where)

⇩

Automatic Thoughts (Hidden goal of anticipated session)

⇩

Assumptions Behind Goal (Motivations, whether just to have fun with others or to relieve sadness, anger, anxiety, etc.)

⇩

Reinforcers (Other personal motivators; support of friends; extra money on hand; parents away)

While most of our responses to events occur with very little prior thinking, or at least unrecognized, prior thinking, when we stop to reflect on how we react, we find that our immediate, emotional reaction, which triggers our behaviour, is dictated by a basic thought. Further, we find that those basic thoughts are reinforced by other, supporting thoughts or circumstances

The Core Methodology of Thinkin' Drinkin'

The core methodology of Thinkin' Drinkin is pretty basic. Essentially, it involves the following sequence of activities:

1. Freeze-frame your automatic thinking before you decide to go into a potentially excessive drinking session. When you have an intention to drink, stop yourself and identify the motivation behind the intention (note: there may be several). Are you tempted by a desire to simply join some people to have fun? Is it to relieve boredom, to mitigate anxiety, to express defiance, to bolster your courage to be argumentative or feisty with someone who has challenged you in some way? By "freeze-frame" I mean stop for a moment and carefully examine what you are thinking regarding your motivation for drinking. The tactic is equivalent to a method in movies or television in which a single image or series of images is stopped, for dramatic effect, to focus in on an important, telling part of the large flow of the movie's story line. Anyway, once you've been able to answer *why* you want to drink, it is a lot easier to determine if it is sensible or not — and to weigh it against other safer or more effective alternatives to meeting your immediate needs, which takes us to the next steps.

2. Identify the desired outcome of the drinking session, including the risks that are likely involved. Try to picture what the outcome of a drinking session motivated by the reason-for-drinking you have identified. For example, if you are angry with someone who you expect to be at the session, do you secretly hope to confront the person and insult them, argue angrily with them or fight them?

3. Assess whether the outcome you anticipate places you or another person(s) at unnecessarily high risk as a result of the drinking session. Realistically assess the possible or even likely outcomes of getting into a drinking session that might lead to negative outcomes, such as an exchange of insults or a fight, or just drinking way too much.

4. Consider whether the drinking session should be avoided altogether or if there are specific ways of behaving that can mitigate the identified risks anticipated as a potential outcome of the session. If you recognize the risks are very high, then you should consider avoiding the session altogether or, if you intend to go through with it, make sure you don't make yourself vulnerable or offensive by drinking too much.

5. TAKE SOME TIME and be sure to CONDUCT THE ABOVE 4 STEPS WHEN YOU ARE THINKING ABOUT YOUR DRINKING AS A GENERAL STRATEGY. In other words, think of the various thoughts and situations that draw you into drinking sessions, and consider whether there are habits of thought that dictate how you drink—and if they seem to lead you to excessive drinking or various forms of, well . . .TROUBLE! If there are, start changing them. You will find that, in various ways, these basic steps are the essential tools that make up the strategies outlined in the next two chapters.

Chapter 10

Thinkin'-*Not*-Drinkin' (Liberating Strategies for Alcoholics, Potential Alcoholics, and Others Who Simply Shouldn't Drink)

Let me repeat: *not everybody should drink alcoholic beverages.* On a temporary basis, pregnant mothers and people on a variety of medications should not drink. Added to that temporary "no-no" list is anybody, while on the job, who is employed in work directly impacting the safety of co-workers, customers, or the public and for which exceptional mechanical, physical or logistical competencies are required.

On a long-term basis, abstaining is on the order board for individuals prone to alcohol-dependence, as well as predictably high risk problem drinkers.

It remains the case that, for most people, alcohol can be sensibly managed, however; with the right approach, it poses no threat.

While the core of this book is devoted to the promotion of sensible drinking management, I also felt the responsibility to suggest solutions to those addicted to alcohol – or rapidly going in that direction – and those with predictably dangerous, embarrassing or otherwise substantially troublesome drinking patterns. In this chapter, I therefore offer up some guidelines to address these problems.

If you recognize that you should personally address the problem of alcohol dependency or extreme stinkin' drinkin,' there's no way around it:

abstinence should be your primary goal. It is possible to adopt a managed drinking strategy. Some have done that very thing and a minority of them have done it successfully. But to be frank, the risks are really too high, so it's probably *not* worth the effort.

Answering the Question: 'Am I an Alcoholic' (i.e., 'Alcohol Dependent')?

The material provided in Chapter 6 of this book can serve as an initial guide to determining if you should or should not practice complete abstinence. That includes considering the DSM-IV classification of alcohol dependence used by most physicians and psychiatrists and as outlined in that chapter.

In case you're still not convinced, try answering the questionnaires provided in the appendix. The scores you get from those tests should provide you with a pretty valid indicator that you are already experiencing alcohol problems that need to be addressed. If this is the case, then it instructs you how to proceed beyond these indicators that you have a problem with alcohol to a test for actual alcohol dependency. If this self-examination suggests that you have or are very likely to acquire an alcohol dependence problem, then you probably should seriously explore the matter with a professional Counsellor—and yes, it is quite possible that an abstinence strategy is your only smart option.

Answering the Question: 'Do I Lose it When I Drink?'

As I noted above, there are also other types of drinkers who should practice abstinence. If, when you drink, you predictably either engage in behaviour that leaves you ashamed the next day or high risk behaviour, then you probably should decide to quit drinking for the long-term. You should also establish a lifestyle that strongly reinforces that choice.

Often, individuals who cleave to bizarre behaviour when they drink suffer from deep, unhealed emotional scars or a psychological disorder that mixes poorly with drinking. If you are counted among these ranks, t is critical that you directly address these unresolved emotional issues.

In addition, you should begin to practice abstinence immediately and, as part of that process, seek professional counselling to address your psychological or emotional issues. The research literature is pretty clear that good counselling can work effectively with clients who are willing to take the counselling process seriously.

Strategic Steps to Achieve Satisfying Abstinence

If you have concluded that your drinking days should be ended, I suggest that you take the following steps:

1. **Examine your values and primary life goals–and determine how alcohol use might compromise them.**

I suggest you start by rereading the previous sections of the book that describe the outcomes of heavy drinking (See Chapter 5, in particular). Next, shift to a concrete self-appraisal of your value priorities and the life goals that you want to achieve (e.g., getting a certain kind of education or training, excelling at a sport, succeeding in a business or job, having a good marriage and being a good parent).Then, I'd like you to consider how continued alcohol abuse comes into conflict with and undermines your priority values and interferes with your achievement of your primary life goals.

Begin by considering the most basic domains of living, and then, with some reflection, identify your basic, core values in each of these domains. Then go on to assign specific goals to be pursued in the service of those core values.

Here's an example of the outcomes of one alcohol abuse client asked to carry out this exercise:

Core Domain Values	(Examples of) Goals Established to Effectively Express my Values
I have a responsibility to care for myself physically (I accept the old adage that says:"My body is a temple that I should respect and honour")	1. I will learn about good nutrition and learn to eat in a healthy way. 2. I will learn about healthy exercise and plan out and implement a physical activity strategy that promotes my physical health. 3. I will learn and intermittently review how alcohol abuse can compromise my health and safety.
I have a responsibility to nurture and care for myself mentally.	1. I will learn about healthy, rational thinking principles and work hard to implement them in the routines of my life. 2. I will learn about and participate in activities that promote my thinking and learning capacities–and apply them to my education (and/or my work). 3. I will learn about stress and how to manage it. 4. I will learn about and intermittently review how alcohol abuse can negatively affect my mental state.
I have a responsibility to create a strong basis in emotional health for myself	1. I will learn the characteristics of mature emotional health and apply them to the management of my own emotions. 2. If any circumstances in my life are creating a great deal of stress that seem to be resulting in emotional pain, anger, sadness or moodiness, I will seek advice from a parent, wise acquaintances, a minister, or a professional Counsellor. With this help, I will try to find the source of the stress and deal with it effectively.

Core Domain Values	(Examples of) Goals Established to Effectively Express my Values
I want to have satisfying, intimate relationships that I will nurture, preserve and respect.	1. When I am getting to know another person with the intent of developing a sense of intimacy, I will treat them in a positive, caring and respectful way—and demand (but earn) the same from them. 2. Within the next ten years I will develop a loving relationship that can potentially lead to a happy, mutually respectful, permanent partnership. 3. I will learn about and intermittently review how alcohol can negatively impact on a solid, healthy love relationship.
I want myself and the people I love and who depend upon me to have a happy, enjoyable life.	If I form a family with a partner: 1. I want to have kids and be an excellent parent. 2. I want to have a life in which myself and my family experience an interesting, enjoyable and active social life. 3. I want to have a life in which myself and my family enjoy a variety of healthy, sometimes challenging, recreational activities. 4. I will review and intermittently revisit the various ways that alcohol abuse can impact negatively on those I love and my capacity to be an effective parent.

Core Domain Values	(Examples of) Goals Established to Effectively Express my Values
I want to contribute to the well-being of my friends, my community and its members and the environment in which I live.	1. I want to be respected by my friends and in my community so that I can play an active role in the community. 2. I want to be a volunteer and perhaps even a leader in organizing important community projects. 3. I want to help the kids in my neighbourhood who are struggling because their parents don't seem to be providing them much love and support. 4. I want to work with people in the community to make sure that a recent redevelopment proposal doesn't go through and decimate our community by running a freeway right through its centre. 5. I want to learn how frequent alcohol abuse can impact on my capacity to achieve all of these goals.
As a rule, I want to be kind to other people.	1. I will learn what "empathy" means, and "sympathy," and attempt to consider other people's needs when they seem to be hurt or would benefit from some assistance. 2. I will be respectful rather than rude to both people I meet for the first time and people I am involved with on an everyday basis. 3. My default position will be to assume that other people are good and, even when they seem a little offensive, I will be kind to them. 4. I want to consider all the ways that those heavy drinking bouts and hangovers can compromise my kindness with other people.

The same client then added another column to the right of the above two column table. In the third column he described how irresponsible drinking could negatively interfere with his primary life goals. Some examples of his results are presented in the table on the next page.

How Drinking Can Mess Up One's Life Goals . . . A Client's Contemplation:

Core Domain Values	(Examples of) Goals Established to Effectively Express my Values	How Abusive Drinking Sabotages my Goals
I have a responsibility to care for myself physically (I accept the old adage that says:"My body is a temple that I should respect and honour")	1. I will learn about good nutrition and learn to eat in a healthy way.	My eating habits get crazy when I drink too much. Pizza, salty snackers-both during the drinking and as part of a hangover.
	2. I will learn about healthy exercise and plan out and implement a physical activity strategy that promotes my physical health.	All the gains I make at the gym get lost in the bar (flabby body; weight gain)
	3. I will learn and intermittently review how alcohol abuse can compromise my health and safety.	I am drinking too much and it is affecting my health in all kinds of ways.

Core Domain Values	(Examples of) Goals Established to Effectively Express my Values	How Abusive Drinking Sabotages my Goals
I have a responsibility to nurture and care for myself mentally.	1. I will learn about healthy, rational thinking principles and work hard to implement them in the routines of my life.	My head gets out of shape when I drink too much. I'm not very rational when I go to the bar too often.
	2. I will learn about and participate in activities that promote my thinking and learning capacities–and apply them to my education (and/or my work).	When I spend too much time at the bar I do get all stressed out and I can't seem to control it.
	3. I will learn about stress and how to manage it.	
	4. I will learn about and intermittently review how alcohol abuse can negatively affect my mental state.	

Core Domain Values	(Examples of) Goals Established to Effectively Express my Values	How Abusive Drinking Sabotages my Goals
I have a responsibility to create a strong basis in emotional health for myself	1. I will learn the characteristics of mature emotional health and apply them to the management of my own emotions.	When I drink and when I drink too much over a few weeks I act pretty irresponsibly and I feel emotionally immature.
	2. If any circumstances in my life are creating a great deal of stress that seem to be resulting in emotional pain, anger, sadness or moodiness, I will seek advice from a parent, wise acquaintances, a minister, or a professional Counsellor. With this help, I will try to find the source of the stress and deal with it effectively.	When I'm drinking too much, I think I can cope with times that things are all wrong, like when someone in my family has suffered a setback. But I can't seem to deal with it very well. I seem to run from the problem by drinking and I'm not very helpful to others and it seems like I'm running from their problems.

Core Domain Values	(Examples of) Goals Established to Effectively Express my Values	How Abusive Drinking Sabotages my Goals
I want to have satisfying, intimate relationships that I will nurture, preserve and respect.	1. When I am getting to know another person with the intent of developing a sense of intimacy, I will treat them in a positive, caring and respectful way—and demand (but earn) the same from them.	I treat my friends and my girlfriend pretty badly when I'm drinking too much.
	2. Within the next ten years I will develop a loving relationship that can potentially lead to a happy, mutually respectful, permanent partnership.	Frankly, I'm not really good to my partner when I'm drinking too much. I get possessive, jealous, and I'm cranky a lot from being drunk and being hung over.
	3. I will learn about and intermittently review how alcohol can negatively impact on a solid, healthy love relationship.	My girlfriend tells me I'm a real jerk when I'm drinking. She says she doesn't even like me sometimes, the way I act and all.

Core Domain Values	(Examples of) Goals Established to Effectively Express my Values	How Abusive Drinking Sabotages my Goals
I want myself and the people I love and who depend upon me to have a happy, enjoyable life.	If I form a family with a partner: 1. I want to have kids and be an excellent parent. 2. I want to have a life in which myself and my family experience an interesting, enjoyable and active social life. 3. I want to have a life in which myself and my family enjoy a variety of healthy, sometimes challenging, recreational activities. 4. I will review and intermittently revisit the various ways that alcohol abuse can impact negatively on those I love and my capacity to be an effective parent.	

Core Domain Values	(Examples of) Goals Established to Effectively Express my Values	How Abusive Drinking Sabotages my Goals
I want to contribute to the well-being of my friends, my community and its members and the environment in which I live.	1. I want to be respected by my friends and in my community so that I can play an active role in the community. 2. I want to be a volunteer and perhaps even a leader in organizing important community projects. 3. I want to help the kids in my neighbourhood who are struggling because their parents don't seem to be providing them much love and support.	

Core Domain Values	(Examples of) Goals Established to Effectively Express my Values	How Abusive Drinking Sabotages my Goals
I want to contribute to the well-being of my friends, my community and its members and the environment in which I live.	4. I want to work with people in the community to make sure that a recent redevelopment proposal doesn't go through and decimate our community by running a freeway right through its centre. 5. I want to learn how frequent alcohol abuse can impact on my capacity to achieve all of these goals.	

Core Domain Values	(Examples of) Goals Established to Effectively Express my Values	How Abusive Drinking Sabotages my Goals
As a rule, I want to be kind to other people.	1. I will learn what "empathy" means, and "sympathy," and attempt to consider other people's needs when they seem to be hurt or would benefit from some assistance.	When I drink, I'm often not very respectful and I tend to get miserable with people if they bother me at all.
	2. I will be respectful rather than rude to both people I meet for the first time and people I am involved with on an everyday basis. 3. My default position will be to assume that other people are good and, even when they seem a little offensive, I will be kind to them. 4. I want to consider all the ways that those heavy drinking bouts and hangovers can compromise my kindness with other people.	I'm not willing to go out of my way for people when I'm drinking a lot. I think it's because I guess this sort of dark attitude takes over and I feel real cynical. I also get irritable and that hardly makes you Mr. Nice Guy.

Now it's your turn.

In the table below, identify your own core values, priority goals and the ways you think heavy drinking will undermine your goals and, as a result, be in an ongoing conflict with your core values.

My Core Values, Goals and the Ways that Heavy Drinking is Likely to Get in the Way of Realizing my Ambitions

Core Domain Values	(Examples of) Goals Established to Effectively Express my Values	How Heavy Drinking will Undermine my Priority Life Goals

Core Domain Values	(Examples of) Goals Established to Effectively Express my Values	How Heavy Drinking will Undermine my Priority Life Goals

NOTE: This matrix doesn't provide a lot of room to write, so you might just take a notepad; create a new matrix that fits your own space needs.

2. **Examine Your Level of Motivation to Change**

Changing difficult habits is not as simple as merely making a decision and then acting on your choice. Sometimes "cold turkey" changes appear to happen that way. Yet when psychologists have carefully studied the processes that accompany dramatic behavioural change, they have found that the matter is somewhat more complicated In most circumstances, change seems to begin at the point at which a little bit of commitment occurs and, with greater degrees of intensity, that commitment grows, eventually translating into a clear-cut decision, which is then transformed into actions that reflect change and supportive behaviours that reinforce that change. Along the way, there are failures of commitment but these are treated as reminders of the dangers of relapse and a clear signal to get back on target with the abstinence strategy.

Since 1984 there have been over 500 research and theory articles dealing with a model of behaviour change described as the "stages of change," first described by psychologists James O. Prochaska, John C. Norcross and Carlo C. DiClemente in application to addictions (1992). The research has examined the changes of behaviour that occur in a variety of problem areas before and after attempts to overcome the problem are made. A total of twelve different types of problem behaviour have been studied, including smoking, lack of exercise, eating a high-fat diet and illegal drug use, as well as problem drinking.

The results of these many studies have shown that the same pattern of change – the "stages" of change — occurred across all behaviour change types considered in the study. These stages can be described as follows:

- *Precontemplation*, which is the stage at which we don't even seriously consider changing a troublesome behaviour.

- *Contemplation*. At this stage, we start to think about changing a behaviour pattern. The main feeling we experience here is ambivalence: we want things to change by we also want them to stay the same.

- *Preparation* is the stage at which we shift beyond our "two minds" about the problem – wanting to overcome it but feeling comfort in keeping things as they are – to a point at which we have made a decision to change in the face of various troubling circumstances. While we still have some reservations about making the change, we have developed a clear commitment to change.

- *Action*. At this stage, we develop a plan to change and, with that commitment we start taking the steps required to make the change.

- *Maintenance*. At this stage we have made the change and we no longer carry out the behaviour of our concern – e.g., heavy drinking – and sustain our commitment to the change.

- *Relapse*. At this stage we end up renewing the troubling behaviour. For our purposes, a problem drinker starts the problem drinking habit again.

Hopefully, the relapse is not long-term; in fact, it is hoped that the individual will:

- *Return to the Maintenance stage*—and the majority do, although full abstinence can involve a number of slips before complete abstinence occurs.

What underlies these "stages of change" is a thinking process that involves weighing costs and benefits. The further along in the movement through the stages towards abstinence one goes, the more benefits emerge to reinforce that very abstinence: better health, more variation in one's lifestyle, greater trust invested in one by other people. At the same time, there are fewer negative consequences, such as morning-after headaches and hangovers, reductions in constant thirst, fewer scary incidents, and fewer embarrassing interactions with people with care about.

In the old disease model of explaining and intervening in alcohol dependency, when someone abandons abstinence and has an evening of heavy drinking, s/he is in need of complete renewal. One is sternly advised that s/he has to start the "recovery" process all over again: a return to "Step 1," as it were. But it *ain't* necessarily so.

More recent, scientifically informed thinking suggests that problem drinking, like any other high risk and intense habit, is **better treated as a slip rather than as full relapse**. The upshot of this conclusion is that the abuser of alcohol is encouraged to see relapse as an unfortunate mistake rather than a major defeat. After all, the reasoning goes, nobody's perfect, mistakes are normal when we're first modifying any problem behaviour that has been a central element of our lifestyle.

In the more current view, the best approach is to treat the relapse incident as a mistake but, rather than immediately starting your change process all over again; you just revisit your rationale for change and return, with greater resolve, to your abstinence strategy. But it doesn't hurt to go over the skill set you have learned and to mobilize activities and friends that support you and encourage your abstinence.

3. **Consider medical and psychological problems you have that might be related to alcohol problems–and get a psychological and physical check-up as part of that consideration.**

I don't want to scare you but it is time to undertake a substantial examination of your psychological and medical status. There are a variety of symptoms of problem drinking, all of which may act as either or both causes (or, better stated, "motivational influences") and effects of the problem. Put yourself in the patient role and, at least initially, act as your own physician and psychologist. Consider the following:

Warning Signs Centred in Your Moods and Emotional Life

1. Do you find yourself really moody a lot of the time?

2. Do you find yourself often teary, frequently given to crying, even thought you find it embarrassing and don't want to?

3. Are you experiencing emotionally painful and stressful family problems or problems with your girlfriend or boyfriend or even just your close friends?

4. Are you experiencing school and/or work-related problems?

5. Have you found yourself despondent, kind of bored with life and, even, on occasion, contemplating suicide?

Pancreas/Spleen Effects

6. Are you experiencing sensitivity or pains just below your ribs, in your lower left abdomen?

Gastrointestinal Problems

Have you:

7. been experiencing stomach pain, including pain during or shortly after meals?

8. recently experienced heartburn with some frequency?

9. been having stomach cramps fairly often?

10. been having digestive problems recently?

11. been vomiting more often than usual lately?

12. been developing a "beer belly" – swelling of the abdomen with fluid?
13. been having problems with your bowel movements, including either constipation *or* diarrhoea?
14. had a sore throat lately?

Metabolism

Have you been experiencing:

15. excessive thirst and frequent urination?
16. excessive and persistent hunger?
17. a craving for sweets?

Liver/Gall Bladder

Have you:

18. a heightened sensitivity and pain in your right abdomen?
19. an enlarged, hardened area in the right part of your stomach area?
20. recently been vomiting blood?

Cognition (thinking)

21. Have you been feeling kind of jittery lately?
22. Has your thinking seemed a little confused lately?

Lungs

Have you been experiencing:

23. frequent colds since the onset of your alcohol dependency?
24. excessive nasal and sinus congestion?

Kidneys and Bladder

Have you been having:

25. pains and cramps in the middle of your back?

26. difficulty when you urinate?

Heart

Have you recently been experiencing:

27. rapid heartbeat, which is sometimes rapid and irregular?

28. chest pains?

29. heart palpitations?

Blood

Have you been experiencing:

30. feelings of weakness and have you been feeling faint?

31. occasional fainting?

Eyes

Have you been having:

32. repeated eye infections?

33. weakened vision, especially at night?

Bones, Joints and Muscles

Have you been experiencing:

34. muscle pain and cramps?

35. frequent broken bones?

36. sharp pain in joints?

37. poor muscle tone and muscle development?

Sex Organs

38. If you are a female, have you experienced an increase in vaginal infections?

39. Have you experienced a decreased sex drive and a decrease in your enjoyment of sex?

Signs of Mental Disturbance

40. Do you experience feelings of jumpiness, of being "on edge"?

41. Do you occasionally – or even frequently — experience loss of memory and general forgetfulness?

42. Have you experienced shooting pains in your extremities?

43. Have you sometimes experienced a loss of coordination?

44. Have you experienced mild to severe tremors?

45. Have you lately being experiencing clouded, confused and illogical thinking?

46. Have you experienced frequent accidents that, when you think about it, might be related to confused thinking and forgetfulness?

General Physical Signs During Advanced Stages

47. Have you developed an observable flushing of the skin (reddening)?

48. Do you have small red blemishes that turn white when you apply pressure to them?

49. Have you experienced an increase in prominently visible red blood vessels in the face and dark red skin blotches?

50. Have you developed circles around your eyes bags under them?

51. Do you have a generally poor skin condition?

52. Would you say that your hair is in poor condition and are you experiencing an increased loss of hair?

    a. Have you experienced steady weight loss lately?

53. Have you experienced steady weight gain lately?

54. Is your voice raspy or hoarse?

55. Does your gag reflex seem more ready to trigger lately?

Seems like overkill, eh!

I know! I know! It is unlikely that most of the items on this list apply to you. But many of them might already and just going through them gives you a good sense of what is in store for you if you continue on the path to intense, alcohol addiction.

Chances are you do have a few of the problems on the list already, however, if you are becoming alcohol dependent. With the information gained from this self-examination, you should seriously consider finding a physician to give you a comprehensive physical examination, paying attention to any of the problems you might have personally identified, as well as other potential alcohol-related problems.

4. Establish a Comprehensive Strategy for Becoming Abstinent

So, if you are a high risk binger or you sense that you are an alcoholic or you are at least on a fast or slow but sure track to alcohol dependency, then you should establish a comprehensive, personalized strategy to work towards and reinforce your abstinence. Some strategies to consider are outlined below. Other initiatives you might consider taking are included in the thinkin' drinkin' materials in the next chapters.

Avoidance Tactics: If abstinence is your goal, you should consider many of the strategies below that allow you to deter yourself from urges and drinking cues. For example, stay away from people, places, and other triggers, such as specific drinking establishments, situations, such as linked recollections of people you enjoy and pleasant parties. Avoid certain music, movies and TV shows that make you want to drink by bringing positive drinking memories to the surface.

Decide on 'Cold Turkey' or 'Phasing Out:' If you have other addictions, you should begin to address them immediately but you should carefully consider whether a lock-step approach that eliminates one addiction at a time or all of them is your best course of action. Good counselling should help you make this choice—and, probably, inpatient treatment ('rehab,' as they say). Having an ongoing relationship with an addictions Counsellor, including a Counsellor-facilitated group can be important.

Join a Support Group: Involvement in a self-help group, whether AA or other groups, such as SOS or RET, can also be excellent supports for recovery and an ongoing support for maintenance of your abstinence program. I personally prefer the latter – SOS or RET — but there is no doubt that the widespread geographic availability, the fellowship and the mentoring (by what AA calls a 'Sponsor') can be a great help once your committed to overcoming your alcohol dependency problem.

Get Active in Sober Recreational Activities: Finding participating in enjoyable and interesting activities on a scheduled and regular basis can be the key to overcoming an addiction, especially if you arrange them at times that you previously used to drink. Alcohol and drug abuse problems are substitute sources of relief from boredom and loneliness and through busy participation in activities with other people, alcohol use simply gets crowded out of your personal recreation time and space.

Learn Effective 'Drink Refusal' Skills: The discussion below, aimed at problem drinkers (non-alcohol dependents), regarding drink refusal skills and the challenge of dealing with former drinking partners and people who will encourage you to drink, will also be of direct value to your strategy.

Avoid Compulsive Drinking Friends

I have come to believe that REAL FRIENDS ARE 'DRY' FRIENDS!

Examine your friendships to determine if they are based almost entirely on drinking companionship or they are sound, mutually supportive relationships that have an easy comfort zone outside of social drinking–and test them. If they can be counted in the first category, abandon them. No matter how hard it may be, find one or more *real* friends, individuals that enjoy you and you enjoy because your values, personality, humour and interests (other than drinking) coincide.

Initially, you should try cutting down on your own drinking or fully abstaining, of course, and assessing what happens. Sometimes your drinking partner's excesses also diminish, simply because of your influence on him or her.

If you trust your drinking partners as friends, you might ask them to help you with your efforts to control your drinking and to help you phase it out of your life.

If you do want help from your friends, you should be very specific about what you are asking them. For example, tell them that you have been drinking too much, it has become a problem in various parts of your life and, for a while, you are going to do other things instead. Ask them to join you to share those activities with you.

Social drinking often has a comforting regularity to it. Ask your friends to meet you for coffee on a regular basis. This can fulfill the same type of need, as millions of upscale coffee spots, like *Starbucks*, have found.

You might also ask your friends to share in an enjoyable, even a health-promoting, regular recreational activity with you.

Note: The above strategy is worth considering, even by non-alcoholic, problem drinkers who intend to acquire a thinkin' drinkin' style.

Defeat Cravings and Anxiety with Relaxation Techniques: The relaxation exercise described below might also be useful. Yoga and learning to meditate can also be of value. Learning to be comfortable with yourself by learning to enjoy spending time alone is extremely important.

Recognize the Losses Incurred by Abandoning Alcohol—and Find Assurance that Alternatives can be Found: It may sound strange but allowing yourself to identify the specific losses incurred as a result of abandoning alcohol use can be helpful. Remember the chapter on the benefits of alcohol: they are real. Beverage alcohol consumption probably became integrated into all kinds of habits other than drinking for you, from get-togethers with friends to a variety of other activities. So realize that there is a loss that can only be overcome with time and substitutions for the pleasures once realized with drinking. Some psychologists argue that these should "grieve" these losses. This may sound a little corny, maybe even a stretch, but for some it may help to take some time alone to cry and mourn what you have lost. Despite what the macho shield that many cling to would suggest, crying can be a very self-constructive and therapeutic activity.

Celebrate Your Decision to Quit: And, finally, celebrate your decision to quit, and celebrate the little gains you make along the way in fighting back your temptations and creating distance from your (former) drinking. Give yourself little rewards for these gains and recruit friends and family members to the reward-giving process. Simple acknowledgement of a week's abstinence by a father, brother or friend can mean a lot.

Anticipate the Possibility of Relapse: As I will repeat and expand upon below, treat a relapse as reminder that you can slip, not as an enormous defeat that proves you can't overcome the problem. Most shifts from alcohol dependency or other forms of addiction, like smoking, involve several attempts before success is realized. So don't be too hard on yourself. Transform a mistake into a learning opportunity. Don't treat it as an indicator of character weakness or as proof that you have an insurmountable, chronic disease: it is a compulsive behaviour that is doing you harm and, in life, there are many compulsions that most of us would be wise to overcome.

Not letting a slip from your abstinence give you an excuse to retreat to your bad drinking habits may be the most important idea that you take from this book. Forgive yourself, write the slip off to experience–and yes, we all do screw up sometimes in most areas of our lives. Most of us fail a few times before we succeed in our attempts to change any undesirable behaviour, so don't let conquering a bad beverage alcohol habit be any different. Think about this: while smokers typically work through many attempts to quit their tobacco habit before they actually succeed, the decline in smoking in North America in recent years has been extremely impressive—and some experts regard smoking as an even tougher addiction to beat than booze, beer and wine.

You should also know that even when teens and young adults have been diagnosed as alcohol dependent, their addictive habit is typically far less intense than when it is left untreated for many years into adulthood. One of the implications of this more limited intensity of addiction in youth is that a medication-free route to abstinence is almost always advisable. There are exceptions to this, of course, such as when explosive, high risk behaviour is predictable, or when a serious mental health problem is involved.

Sometimes, Support from Medications Really is Needed

For those attempting to overcome a dependency on alcohol who are meeting with repeated failure, including those whose efforts are being frustrated by a mental health problem, medications can sometimes be helpful.

There are a number of prescription drugs on the market that can help individuals overcome alcohol dependency, as there are medications to address mental health issues. As the word 'prescription' makes explicit, you need a diagnosis and piece of paper from your physician to legally secure and safely use medications. Your job is to consult with a physician – getting a second opinion is advisable as well – and then take the prescription to a pharmacist, making sure that you have the money or insurance to pay for it. In Canada, such a prescription would be automatically covered by public health insurance.

There are two common types of medications that might be prescribed to support an abstinence goal. One class of medications are those that are used to reduce cravings by making the drinking experience unpleasant, even repulsive. The other types are medications that help you tackle other psychological conditions that influence substance abuse or complicate or are complicated by the use of mood-modifying alcohol use.

Physicians who work with addictive disorders warn us that, for many people who have become addicted to alcohol, it is simply not safe to just have them abruptly quit drinking: to quit, "cold turkey," as the saying goes. Abrupt termination of an intense and persistent drinking habit can result in what is a very medically dangerous withdrawal syndrome.

Approximately 95 percent of people who enter treatment for alcohol dependency have mild to moderate withdrawal symptoms, including agitation, trembling, disturbed sleep, and lack of appetite. In 15 percent to 20 percent of these cases, people with moderate symptoms, brief seizures and hallucinations may occur, but they do not progress to full-blown *delirium tremens*. If you are one of these individuals, it is likely that you will be treated as an outpatient, unless you enter into a private rehabilitation centre.

There are now quite effective drugs that can be used as part of withdrawal. These can do much to promote safety and relieve the discomfort of withdrawal. Whatever the case, these medication supports are only available through a licensed physician. (See Appendix A for a brief description of the medication options).

Once through that withdrawal period, some patients may require continuous treatment with other medications.

All of the medications commonly prescribed are relatively safe. Used under medical supervision, they ensure that an alcohol-dependent patient will be able to stop using the alcohol in a relatively easy and safe way as the alcohol is cleansed from the body.

Chapter 11

The Thinkin' Drinkin' Strategy for Potential Problem Drinkers (i.e., Most of You)

It is time to consider what I call the *Thinkin' Drinkin'* strategy per sé: the strategy at the heart of this book. This is the approach to drinking that most of you should seriously consider because it is safe and sensible in many ways.

Let me repeat my statement that the vast majority of beverage alcohol users are potential problem drinkers, at least on occasion, unless they have a planned approach to drinking which they pursue with consistent resolve. Unless you have a specific plan to help you select when you drink, with whom you drink, and how much you drink, chances are you are going to screw up at some point and, in the process, place yourself or others in harm's way.

In this chapter, the *Thinkin' Drinkin'* strategy is outlined. It is targeted on those of you who are not at high risk of either alcohol dependency or predictably dangerous, recurrent binge drinking, both of which are indicative of the need for abstinence. But do remember, even one drinking binge can be disastrous.

I invite you to follow the action steps below. These steps should lead you to becoming a sensible, moderate drinker throughout your life. Obviously, you will have to customize them, at least a little, to suit your particular needs and circumstances.

Defining Thinkin' Drinkin'

Before I take you through what amounts to a guide to writing your rational drinking plan set out below, I want you to consider what sensible, safe drinking really is. Before you develop a plan to follow, you have to define the purpose of your plan. Of course, such a definition can vary but let me give you a hand by sharing *my* version of rational drinking. You can then modify it to suit your personal inclinations, tastes and circumstances.

For me, thinkin' drinkin' is moderate, non-risky, appropriate, healthy and pro-social drinking that avoids thoughts, circumstances and people that trigger temptations to drink to the point of impairment and to enact behaviour that would occur during a state of sobriety. Let me parse that statement.

By "moderate" drinking I mean non-excessive beverage alcohol consumption that does not push you beyond your personal blood alcohol impairment threshold.

Thinkin' drinkin' does not place one – or others — at elevated risk because the intentions of the drinker are positive and healthy rather than based in troubles or extremities of mood.

Thinkin' drinkin' does not involve drinking until you get drunk. You do not drink as fast as you can and as much as you can. You do not drink with the intention of getting drunk…

Thinkin' drinkin' also insists that you remain fully in charge of your own behaviour during a drinking session. You do not let your darker moods, your hurt emotions or your anger—and not your libido (your sexual urges)—rule your behaviour.

Thinkin' drinkin' is a drinking style that varies with and is appropriate to different situations. It could limit you to a glass or two of champagne at a gathering celebrating a graduation, a sports victory, or an academic accomplishment. It could be three glasses over several hours during a get together at a home or bar for a renewal of acquaintanceship among old friends (assuming you are aware of legal limits for driving).

The drinking style I am promoting also involves what I call "rational avoidance," which refers to a conscious effort to ignore those happy or unhappy memories that seem to encourage you to drink beyond your safe limit. It also involves avoiding people who are too frequently encouraging you to go drinking with them. Thinkin' drinkin' is determining how much you will drink on the basis of pre-determined limits, not on the basis of the urgings of those you are with who repeatedly prompt you by saying: "Ah come on, let's have another one!"

Rational avoidance also involves consciously staying away from groups, bars and parties that are either centred on getting drunk or intrinsically laden with the type of interpersonal conflict that almost inevitably leads to emotional confrontations or physical fights.

Thinkin' drinkin' is sensible drinking and it is a drinking frequency that is limited over time. It is not drinking everyday or every week. It is drinking that is consciously limited; it is limited in the amount consumed per session, in the frequency of drinking episodes you participate in, and in terms of the amount that you allow it to crowd out other more important and enjoyable alternatives in your life.

Thinkin' drinkin' also discourages you from supporting beverage alcohol use at every social get together or formal or celebratory event that you attend. Drinking should be an occasional indulgence.

Whatever the occasion on which you drink, if you are drinking sensibly, the alcohol itself should not be the primary focus of the situation. If you are drinking for the sake of drinking, you almost inevitably get drunk and are prone to risky, stupid behaviour.

Thinkin' drinkin' does not undermine relationships, resulting in your saying things to intimates, friends, acquaintances or authority figures that you later regret. Nor does it sacrifice your reputation as a solid, stable, reliable, trustworthy and helpful friend, student, team member or employee.

Thinkin' drinkin' is also learning to avoid drinking altogether when you have more important things to attend to, such as an exam the next day, when you are on a 15 minute break from work time or when you are anticipating a long shift on a risky job site the next day.

Okay, it's your turn.

Take 10 minutes or so to describe the kind of drinking style you want and, in concise, point form, describe the elements of that style in the box below.

In my opinion, a safe and sensible drinking style is characterized by the following:

Action Tactics for Thinkin' Drinkin'

STAGE 1: REVIEW, RENEW AND FIRM UP YOUR PRIORITIES

During Stage 1, I want you to engage in a reflective conversation with yourself — a self-reflective conversation – regarding your priorities and the place of drinking in the life space those priorities will create.

REVIEW STRATEGY 1: Establish a Drink Free Prep-Time Period.

The first stage of the thinkin' drinkin' strategy begins with what I call a "Drink Free Time Zone," which is 3-6 weeks in which you avoid alcohol so that you are best able to pay some serious attention to your long term needs and the ways that alcohol affects them. This period should not only help you to deal with alcohol but will also allow you take a serious inventory of where you want to go with your life in the future. If you find that you are desperate for a drink the entire time the entire time you are wholly abstinent, you probably should seek the professional help of an addictions Counsellor, clinical social worker or clinical psychologist who offers relevant counselling services. You are probably not a good candidate for the thinkin' drinkin' strategy and you should consider instead for the abstinence goal strategy described above (See the *thinkin'—not—drinkin' strategy*).

If you have been drinking a lot recently, you may also want to undertake a detoxification process that commits you to cleaning out your body of toxins – the garbage we accumulate from junk foods and regular meals with heavy sugar and fat content – and involves some healthy exercise. The simple contrast between a period of heavy drinking and what it really feels like to have a body that is being treated well is itself an important motivator for self-planned health.

REVIEW STRATEGY 2: Commit to shaping good drinking habits.

Revisit the discussion of habits (see Chapter 9), both good and bad. This should help you to gain a firm understanding of your capacity to shape your own life course by identifying positive and negative habits and by consciously creating a healthy lifestyle dominated by healthy, constructive habits. The core points made in that chapter are as follows:

- ✓ Human beings have to learn almost all of their behaviour patterns. Unlike most animals, we rely on learning through formal language communication and through various other messages conveyed through non-verbal communication.

- ✓ Human beings form families, communities, societies to support the long period required to socialize and educate their dependent young, to produce and distribute food, clothing and shelter, to organize water collection and manage the disposal of waste. They also organize collectively to protect their fold from the predation of other people and other animals.

- ✓ To organize human groups efficiently, we establish habits, most of which are referred to as norms and some of these norms are give higher status as moral guidelines and as laws, which are given the weight of force when they are violated.

- ✓ We human beings are habit-forming animals and we must be to get along and survive as families and in our communities and societies as a whole.

- ✓ Some of our habits grow out of reaction to the norms, sometimes even the laws, and ultimately we also have the free will to modify many of our own personal habits and to deviate from the norms.

- ✓ Norms and personal habits can vary in terms of their benefit to you and others. There are good norms and bad norms. At one time driving while intoxicated was norm and we would probably all agree that that was a bad norm. Co-operative protocols and showing respect to each other and showing special patience and respect for elders is probably an uncontested good norm.

- ✓ There are also good personal habits and bad ones.

Over time, your sensible drinking will become habitual. I've written about the many ways that drinking behaviour can become a very bad habit, sometimes even a fatal one. Thinkin' drinkin' is about making drinking a good habit.

REVIEW STRATEGY 3: Seriously reflect on your priorities and consider how careless drinking might stymie them.

In Strategy 3 of Stage 1, I want you to consciously consider what is important to you and then to assess how a careless drinking strategy compares with a rational drinking strategy in terms of supporting your primary life interests.

Drinking alcoholic beverages does not occur in a vacuum; instead, it is implicated in many areas of your life. It affects various slices of what I call a person's "health pie," which includes all other major dimensions of living—from your physical health through your emotional health and on to your spiritual and social health. I tend to think in terms of systems and their interactions because it reminds me that in life generally, everything is part of several systems and both the parts of specific systems and the systems that make up the larger, universal environment, affect and are effected by each other.

To truly get a strong handle on your primary interests, consider what work you must do to make sure the following are in good shape (Get a pen or pencil and paper and make notes of relevance to each of the following areas of healthy [or unhealthy] living):

- Your *physical health* is being handled lovingly and with a nurturing attitude with the help of (i) good nutrition (ii) plenty of exercise and (iii) securing immediate medical attention for any current and past physical disorders—and getting regular check-ups as a preventive measure.

- You are taking your *emotional health* seriously and if you are experiencing emotional pain that is troubling you, it might make sense to see a professional Counsellor. Past trauma, persistent anger, feelings of depression, extreme inadequacy in any area, and suicidal or homicidal thoughts should all be taken very seriously.

- Your *cognitive health* (the quality of your thinking style) in general is being taken care of, which means that if you should start considering how you think before you act and whether or not that thinking helps you or hinders you in achieving what you want. You should also ask yourself: Is there some aspect of my thinking that impedes my efforts to accomplish what I want to in school, at work, in sports, in relationships.

- Your *social health* is satisfying, including having opportunities for and being comfortable with solitude or, in other words, spending time alone and doing things on your own; developing supportive and satisfying family ties; having supportive friends whose company you enjoy and who do not pressure you to do things that might be resistant to, like treating other people poorly or spending too much time at the bar or taking drugs. It also means that you should develop a support network of parents, friends, relatives, and peers, as well as professionals in helping roles, such as guidance Counsellors, social workers in the neighbourhood or at school, and even police.

- Assess your *sexual health*. Is your sexual identity – whether 'straight,' 'bisexual' or 'gay' – clearly defined in your own head and are you comfortable with that identify. Take time to explore that question and make sure that the confusion and anxiety surrounding the issue is not encouraging tormented drinking and careless sexual experimentation.

- Consider the current and desired state of your *educational well-being*. How well have you realized your education and training goals to date? What are your deficiencies in this regard? What would you most like to accomplish in the education and training fields of your choice?

- What is the career (or careers) that you would most like to pursue? What must you do to establish an education, training and career mobility path (how and what to do to climb to achieve your ambitions) that leads to a *satisfying work life*. Consider not only the education and training you have described in Item 5 above but also the on-the-job relations, activities and employer expectations that you must meet if you are to successfully move along your career path.

- Also consider your *spiritual health*. Whether spirituality is conceived of as being referenced to a major religion or a spiritual movement, or as a process of nourishing your inner self, spirituality appears to be an extremely important aspect of being human. For me, spirituality is about the unique potential each of us has been given to live constructively and happily in harmony with our selves, other people and nature. Spirituality is about our awareness of this potential and the work we undertake to realize this potential. Whatever your individual take on spirituality, this aspect of being human is an important element of a sober, constructive lifestyle and it must be attended to.

- Consider your social conscience, by which I mean your *altruistic health* or, in other words, the manner and extent to which you pay back society and the environment for your own good fortunes. Find some activities that assist the community as a whole or its less fortunate members in particular. By investing your time, energy and sense of purpose in the well-being of others, you inevitably push aside your time and your interest in less responsible activities, like wild and crazy drinking sessions.

Next, on the following page, complete the following exercise:

In the left column of the table provided, write down one or more statements of purpose or specific ambitions (make them concrete goals if you can) in each of the 8 areas and the types of accomplishments you would like to achieve in response to each purpose you have identified.

Next, to the right of each purpose statement, list the ways that out-of-control drinking is likely to frustrate your accomplishments.

Finally, to the right of that list of barriers, identify the ways that a lifestyle in which drinking is controlled will support your attempts to accomplish your goals.

After completing the table, lie down, listen to some music or go for a walk or some other quiet activity that enables serious, private thoughts. Have the table in hand, look at it a few times. Then ask yourself whether or not a rational drinking strategy is important to you?

[*NOTE*: The space in the table is pretty small so you might want to simply use a larger notepad and take more time thinking this through.]

Stinkin' vs. Thinkin' Drinkin' Matrix

Statement of Primary Life Goals (by Life Dimension)	How out-of-control drinking would frustrate my accomplishment in each area	How controlled drinking would help me accomplish my goals
Your physical health		
Your emotional well-being		
Your cognitive strength (how well your thinking works)		
Your social life (including your sexual life)		
Your educational well-being		
Your career development		
Your spiritual well-being (i.e., your comfort with your ultimate beliefs, whether religious, agnostic or atheistic)		
Your contributions to other people and the community as a whole		

Stage 2: Develop a Practical, Generalized *Thinkin' Drinkin'* Strategy.

Now I want you to establish and follow through on a strategy. The scenarios framed below, when the script instructions are followed and when taken together, comprise a thinkin' drinkin' strategy.

ACTION STRATEGY 1: Taper your drinking down

After your period of initial abstinence is over, you should develop a long-term plan to reduce its frequency.

Go back over the few weeks prior to your period of abstinence and try to ascertain the numbers of times per week you drank and how many drinks you had. Then develop a plan for reducing the number of drinking session per week and the number of drinks per session for a given period.

Let's say you estimate that in the month prior to your period of abstinence you were drinking approximately twice a week and the number of drinks varied from 3 to 7 per session. A good plan might be to look at the next month by drinking no more than 5 times, only once a week with one exception, and no more than 3 drinks per session over a 3 hour period. That month might be followed by a once a week drinking maximum and no more than 2 drinks over 3 hours (rotated with another beverage [water, pop, coffee, etc.]).

ACTION STRATEGY 2: Learn drink refusal skills (Learn to say 'no' without making it a big deal).

Refusing any or too many drinks is a key to self-managing your drinking. Acquire some phrases and gestures and actions that you can use in refusing drinks, and rehearse these scenes until you've got them down and your delivery is smooth and confident. Learn them during your period of abstinence, and after. Being able to say no is a critical skill for those attempting to be abstinent or for those simply trying to control when, where, and how much they want to drink. The greatest difficulty is posed by familiar drinking acquaintances who will find it a little upsetting that they've lost a drinker they could formerly rely on, and they are likely to test you.

If a host at a party or someone you don't know very well asks you if you want to drink, chances are saying "No thanks" is pretty easy and is unlikely to meet with an attempt to get you to change your mind, other than a single, unassertive, "You sure?"

On the other hand, when a person is very familiar with you and surprised that you're not drinking, you are probably best off to be forthright about limiting your drinking tonight, and explaining why. A little explanation is probably in order, so that you don't turn off your acquaintances entirely. Saying that you've got an exam or athletic event in the morning or you're trying to cut back as part of a diet can be useful. Ultimately, you want to enlist them in your drinking control strategy, so take a bit of time to convince them that what you're doing is important to you. If they simply can't accept this change in you, then it's probably time to start avoiding them. They ain't a real friend!

Avoid rational explanations with the guy or gal who is already tipsy or drunk or who wants desperately to get drunk later on. Just say emphatically that you can't tonight and quickly seek other company.

To make it easier on yourself at a party, you might have a dark cola or a ginger ale in your hand most of the time so the offers of a drink never come up.

ACTION STRATEGY 3. Learn to manage your personal temptations to indulge in a binge drinking session.

If you have been a pretty regular drinker, try to become an occasional drinker only, and you can best support that goal by learning to manage your urges, which may be pretty frequent, especially during your period of self-imposed abstinence. Think about ways of taking a detour from your urges by supplanting them with other activities. After a while, these detours become habits and avoiding drinking episodes comes to dominate, so that when you do go for a drink, you really enjoy it: it is a treat rather than a bad habit that is dragging down so many other aspects of your life. Instead of going out to the bar, find alternatives:

- If you are feeling stressed and you think a good session of getting wasted might be a good idea, stop yourself, count to 10, and then consider dealing with the immediate urge by engaging in a good relaxation exercise (See Exhibit 1 below).

- If you have a regular time when you drink, substitute another enjoyable or challenging activity for that regular time so that the feeling of emptiness or loneliness that comes when you abandon the "drinking hour" is basically pushed off your radar. For example,

    - You might go to a sports event with friends, a movie or get a video out to watch at home.

    - Seek out a friend whose company you really enjoy and go for a coffee at Starbucks or a good local coffee shop for a good "shooting the shit" type of conversation.

    - Have a round of safe but exciting sex (its way better than getting drunk)—or a reasonable facsimile.

    - Get together with someone or, on your own, play some video games.

    - Find a partner to play a game of golf or another "twosome" sport.

    - Get together with a group of friends who are playing cards or an athletic activity like ball hockey or basketball (as part of either, you might drink lightly [i.e., *during* the card game] or winding down, after the team sport). Getting involved in sports or recreational events that take place at the same time you usually go for a drink can be a great way to reduce an overly robust drinking habit. A serious commitment to a sport, with realistic but increasingly challenging personal performance goals can be very helpful for deterring your tendency to get involved in heavy drinking when there is a gap in your schedule.

- Catch up on your homework or some personal tasks that you haven't attended to, like maintaining or upgrading your bike or car.

- When you are really torn between wanting to do some serious drinking and knowing the time or situation isn't appropriate, then you might try carrying out a relaxation exercise before you make your choice. My experience is that, after the calmness that comes with such an exercise, my decisions seem to be far wiser than when I am anxiously arguing with myself about choices.

ACTION STRATEGY 4: Consciously address any emotional and sexual anxieties and confusions that might encourage careless drinking.

Ongoing mental or sexual discomfort and confusion couple very poorly with drinking. There is no point in trying to develop a sensible drinking strategy if unresolved emotional and sexual issues are powerful motivators of your careless drinking activity. It is essential that you address these matters directly, while simultaneously working on a sensible drinking strategy.

Remember, drinking is a CNS depressant, not a stimulant that will produce euphoria. While drinking might initially give you a warm feeling and positive high, you should realize that a combination of depression and alcohol can create very self-destructive types of thought patterns, including enhanced aggression or self-destruction of suicidal ideas. So you should find alternatives to drinking when you are depressed. For example, turn to a parent, another trusted adult, or a friend, and talk the depression through; if it persists, arrange to see a Counsellor who can treat you for the problem (sometimes, this may require medication) or teach you the skills to overcome the depression.

If you are drinking to relieve anxiety about a circumstance in your life or a threat of some kind, again, drinking is simply not advised. It is the worst kind of pill: it encourages you to pursue a course of action that is likely to create more trouble for you than the anxiety associated with your motivation to drink. Common examples include anxiety about basic social interaction, mustering the courage to ask a member of the opposite sex out on a date, or confronting someone who is bullying you or challenging you to a fight.

Here's some basic strategies to address anxiety:

1. Carefully examine your anxiety, how it affects you, and its source: the circumstances that trigger it and the specific cues within those circumstances (e.g., circumstance: encountering a parent who you expect to always be angry with you; cues: your cell phone ring; the door of your bedroom that makes you think that a loud knock or an abrupt entry by the parent may come anytime).

2. Explore the self-help literature regarding your anxiety and develop methods to eliminate it and try those things that seem to make sense.

If self-help fails you,

3. try talking to a school Counsellor or a Counsellor available through a public or private sector service. Lacking your own funds and not having a parent willing to fund your counselling is often a problem but your school Counsellor might be able to help by referring you to a publicly supported counselling service.

ACTION STRATEGY 5: Anticipate what you expect at a drinking session—and assess your motivation for participating.

Again, think in advance about the temptations that might be in place in a situation you will be involved with in which people are drinking and make your plans accordingly. If you feel the pressure will be too great to get drunk with old friends, then you might avoid going to the party. Review and again rehearse your drink refusal skills. Think about who will be attending and who will be less likely to try to persuade you to drink heavily.

Know your motivation–and know when your motivation doesn't mix with drink.

Thinkin' Drinkin'

Extensive research now tells us that one of the most significant influences on how excessively we drink and what we do during and after a drinking episode is the motivation we take into a drinking session.

What the research suggests is that *why* we are drinking leads to relatively predictable outcomes. If you intend to get drunk, most often you will; if you intend to stay sober, again, you probably will—if your intentions are clear. If you are not sure why you are drinking – you just go along for the ride with friends – then your motivation is companionship and, often, your need to be one with the group allows the group to provide you with your motivation to drink. Unfortunately, drinking peers often have either potentially destructive motivations for drinking or unclear motivations that shift over a drinking episode in reaction to conversation and encounters. This may result in you leaving the drinking session early or proceeding to tipsiness or on to the great abyss, flat-out drunkenness. Thus to reduce risks of over-drinking and careless, hostile or other injurious behaviour, you should:

Always know *why* you are drinking in advance of the drinking session—never just go along for the ride, without a clear idea of why you are going.

If you are drinking to modify your mood in a celebratory way, place limits on your level of intoxication and find a way of reinforcing the maintenance of that limit (a pact with a friend; a ride or a cab arranged to pick you up at a party at a particular time). Warning: Be honest and deadly serious with yourself about this one. If you have the experience of high risk drinking as a pattern in your past, find another way to celebrate. You're much more likely to live to see another day and celebrate again. By high risk drinking, I'm referring to frequently or even occasionally drinking to the point of blacking out, driving while drinking, getting in fights, or getting beaten up because you place yourself in dangerous social circumstances.

As I've suggest above, if you are drinking to relieve depression, or to address deep emotional o sexual anxieties, don't! Address these other issues in other ways.

SO REMEMBER, PRACTICE FREEZE-FRAMING YOUR THOUGHTS ABOUT *WHY* YOU ARE TEMPTED TO GO DRINKING, every time the occasion arises or you yourself decide you want to go drinking. Eventually it, too, will become a habit—a good habit!

ACTION STRATEGY 6: Associate with friends who support your sensible drinking strategy.

It is also important to examine who you are drinking with. Buried in the choices you make regarding your selection of drinking partners and acquaintances lies a motivation that may lead to trouble. This scene involves finding friends who might drink but don't get drunk, practice sobriety as a principle or abstinence, and start avoiding stinkin' drinkers—and if and when you do decide to drink, choose moderate drinking partners.

Some people with whom you might drink tend to discourage drinking to excess, others encourage it. With some partners, you might have differences which, when uninhibited, you might be moved to say something or do something you might later regret.

Let's be honest! You know it's not going to work with some people that you ask to abstain with you or practice limited drinking as a principle–and some of these type of people will really try to persuade you to spend a lot of time at a bar or sitting having a drinking at home or at their place. In these situations, you might just choose to avoid former drinking partners. By the way, you might treat the willingness of people to help you with your drinking problem as a "dry friendship" test—or even a "real friendship" test. If these "so called friends" aren't willing to support you or even to join you, maybe it's time to disregard them as keepers.

Those people with whom we spend most of our time, those people we consider our friends, are also typically the people we most often drink with. Those relationships centred on drinking often turn out to be distorted by the actual dynamics of drinking interactions. Unfortunately, when put to the test, they turn out to *not* be friendships at all.

In looking back, I can remember literally dozens of people with whom I drank frequently and heavily that I have completely lost contact with and with whom I have never had the urge to resuscitate my relationship.

Others I have abandoned or have abandoned me because their drinking is annoying or troubling for me but I wish it were different. I miss many of them. We had some precious times. However, I have to put things in perspective. Their behaviour threatens my emotional health and I've got to be practical about this matter.

One's memory stores, when opened, contain all kinds of regrettable statements, going both ways between ourselves and others, things we would like to forget and triggers to memory-laden emotional pain. Reviving them just doesn't seem to make sense. Were these relationships, born, nurtured and sustained by drink, really friendships at all? Maybe they began that way but, over time, they turned sour. I had come to recognize that many of my drinking friends mutually encouraged each other to bond almost entirely through the companionship of drinking, which all too often led to getting drunk and being hung over the next morning. This is not a rare experience: it is very common, perhaps even typical of problem drinkers.

Exhibit 1

A STRESS-RELIEVING RELAXATION EXERCISE

To undertake this stress-relieving, relaxation exercise, you should find a quiet place in which you can sit alone for a while without any interruptions from people or intrusions any kind. The room should be big enough for you to lie down in and stretch your arms.

If you have some physical impediment to lying down, it can also be done from a chair. You might want to use some smooth and relaxing instrumental music to play in the background. Also, make sure the room is warm (but not too hot) and that it has a soothing visual look. Blocking exterior light with closed curtains and lighting candles or using some small lights with different colours can create a very supportive effect.

Begin by sitting comfortably on the floor or in a chair. If you are flexible, a sitting yoga position with legs partly or wholly crossed can be an excellent starting point.

If it is possible to dim the lights in the room, do so. Then follow these steps:

1. Begin by breathing deeply and slowly for about 30 seconds.

2. When this 30 second period is finished, strongly exhale, making a whooshing sound, then, for about 10 seconds, breathe normally.

3. Relax your posture. For those who can, shift from a sitting position to a lying position.

4. With your eyes open, again begin to breathe deeply but slowly, then close your eyes.

5. After a few breaths, think about a favourite, calming and comforting image: It could be visual, such as a landscape, a memory of a great day at Grandpa's farm, the face of a warm, consoling person, such as a mother, grandmother, or close friend; it could even be your most recent memory of the room you're in if the lighting conveys a pleasant and soothing feeling (*Note*: You could simply open your eyes to refresh this memory for a second).

6. Now tell yourself that you are truly feeling comfortable, relaxed and devoid of all foreign thoughts: your mind is inactive, your only feel comfort.

7. Now, tell yourself, as you continue to breathe deeply and slowly, that you can hear the lapping flow of a small waterfall in a creek.

8. If you are lying down, you should stretch your arms and legs out and then back so that your legs are straight and your arms are at your sides.

9. Again, for those who are lying down, beginning with your feet, breathe in while tensing your feet and then relax the tension as your breath out. Slowly continue this for your calves, thighs, pelvis, abdomen, hands, forearms, biceps, triceps, shoulders, neck and face. Depending on your physical condition, you may be able to do the same exercise sitting. If you can't, you can just do the exercise while concentrating on each body part, imagining that you feel pressure from each. When you're finished, take three very deep breaths (inhale/exhale) and then relax completely, thinking of nothing, for at least 30 seconds (up to 2 minutes if you can retain a meditative state).

This method works by reducing your level of consciousness in a step-by-step fashion. Gradually it disengages you from a sense of sight, sound and then touch and your heart rates slows down. Your mind relaxes and becomes far less active. Using this method, with practice, you will be able to relax very quickly.

Here are some things you can do to deal pressures issued by "drinking buddies" to drink more than you want to:

- Determine in advance why you want to drink with someone–and reject situations that might get unpleasant or nasty.

- Avoid doing any drinking with someone with whom, in the past, you have had an extremely pleasant, emotionally exciting intimacy with that was almost entirely framed by excessive drinking. Trying to renew that excitement will almost inevitably lead to renewed bouts of excessive drinking. The best way to deal with this is to try to convince this person that you'd like to start getting together with them again, but never for drinking.

- If the potential drinking partner is likely to keep their own drinking under control and to encourage you to do the same, then you might well proceed with confidence–at least if your own limits are set!

- If you hold a grudge against the individual, then avoid drinking with him or her. Determine a better way to share your concerns with them, and resolve the unresolved issue. Too many people live their lives with regrets over what they said "while soused" to an intimate, a family member, a friend, a former teacher, or a present employer. And too many people have died from grudges taken into drinking bouts.

- Find a drinking partner that sets limits on his or her drinking and maintains that set point–or, in the absence of an appropriated drinking partner, refrain entirely from drinking until you meet someone.

ACTION STRATEGY 7: Learn to act out the positive aspects of a modified mood when you are sober.

Drinking can be fun. The positive side of that "buzz" is a benign, uncomplicated, relaxed state of good humour and goofiness. You can achieve some of that by willing it alive. If you want to achieve that state of mind that often comes with being a little tipsy when you either have had no drinks (but are with drinkers) or when you are drinking but not impaired, learn to replicate the pleasant elements of that desired state of "tipsiness." It's a matter of focusing on the experience, especially the pleasant elements, of a mild high, remembering it, and then reconstructing it through imitation. You'll find that drinking partners and party-goers bent on having a good time don't really care if their company is drunk or not, they just want people around them to pump them up, to help them feel relaxed, a little giddy and "in the party mood." If you present yourself in a way that ramps up those outgoing, happy and fun aspects of your hidden personality (qualities that are part of most of us, however hidden they might typically be), then it's likely that you'll satisfy the most robust of revellers at a party–and those you don't are probably a little over the top with their expectations anyway.

ACTION STRATEGY 8: Learn to be smart in dealing with confrontations.

Unfortunately, there is a tendency to use booze to firm up our intestinal fortitude. Why? Because the toxicity of alcohol numbs or perceptions and sensitivity to our own safety and the safety of others. It gives us tunnel vision and, by reducing our capacity to think about consequences, it makes us far dumber than we normally are. Usually the bravado that is oiled by drink produces regrettable results. Instead, learn to avoid confrontations when you drink. People who are drinking have a tendency to say really stupid things and do stupid things that they later regret–and sometimes regret enormously. If you have something that you desperately want to say, figure out an appropriate way of saying it – with due consideration for the consequences and the feelings of the other person — rehearse it, find the right context, and say it. To borrow a phrase from the Latin, "It is chickenshit" to need booze to say what's on your mind. And many people argue convincingly that physical confrontations under the influence of alcohol are even dumber and more cowardly than verbal aggression boosted by inebriation.

If you have a problem with someone that cries out for resolution in your emotional wiring, then figure out a sober and rational way of solving it. It may be that you just want to tell somebody how their actions hurt you or it may demand a well-reasoned argument to make the point. It might also require, for safety's sake, that you put the matter aside because you know the individual is unreasonable and, in some cases, a confrontation with them is dangerous. Why let them get you again?

It is true that the lowered inhibitions that come with a lengthy beer session might make you more brazen and can dull the pain of a punch or kick; it also blunts your thinking and impairs your coordination. Most people fight far better when they are sober and, more important, most people simply don't get into physical fights when they aren't drunk.

But it is important that, just like you should have a strategy for managing your drinking behaviour, you should also have a strategy for managing confrontations and for self-defence.

Managing Trouble, Safely

To avoid the challenges of a physical confrontation when you are drinking, you should have a phased strategy before you even consider engaging in fisticuffs. You might consider the following:

- ✓ If someone tries to provoke you, ask them why their challenge is directed at you and say that you don't intend to fight, if that's what they're after. You might add a phrase that encourages them to calm down, perhaps join you or your table rather than getting into something unpleasant.

- ✓ If the provocation persists, repeat that you don't intend to get into a fight. If you are at a party, you might indicate that you are going to leave to avoid any trouble. If you are at a bar, you would do well to call upon management or a bouncer to intervene before any physical altercation begins. You might also discretely leave the scene if you can get some interference run on the bully that will divert him while you leave.

- ✓ If the individual persists and you can't avoid the confrontation, you might ask friends to contain the individual while you escape.

- ✓ If you do decide that, all things considered, self-defence is the only realistic option, be sure to figure out if the individual has a weapon or ready access to something like a pool clue that could be a weapon, then change your mind and escape as soon as possible. If it's a bare knuckles situation and you are prepared to deal with it directly, then you should probably attempt to immobilize the individual with a basic martial arts hold until he tires and people can come to your aid. If you are going to strike the individual, try to do so in a fashion that ends the confrontation quickly.

- ✓ Avoid humiliating the person who confronts you. If you can, attempt to make amends with the individual. There are always those who hold grudges, and they may want to come after you again and again to settle the old score, making your life miserable with further threats and altercations.

ACTION STRATEGY 9: Commit to staying away from high risk drinking locations

Where you drink (the location) matters. In fact, it really matters. We all know this but somehow we rarely give enough consideration to the enormous impact of the setting on the outcomes of the drinking session.

Built into our notions of drinking venues is the idea that some places are fixed in the public "mind's eye" as an outlet for drunkenness (picture a college bar or a bar near a large factory that is a Friday after work destination, or the house of a family, individual or group of young people notorious for regular drinking or wild parties). And yes, there are other places that drinking might take place but are viewed as drink-free zones or at least drunk-free zones drinking is limited but excesses are truly discouraged. In the latter instance, think of venues allowing a single drink or two on occasion, such as churches, where sacraments are shared or church or community halls where socials are held; schools, where drinking is normally prohibited, even if the PTA may holds a wine and cheese party to honour long-time school volunteers. In addition, think of most businesses, public offices, and many homes, where drinking to the point of excess is a clearly defined "no-no." In general, civility rather than the careless exuberance that tends to accompany heavy drinking are the rule in such places.

By contrast, some locations, such as "tough" bars function almost as invitations to trouble, as expressed in the form of glowering eyeballs between the people at different tables, rough talk, challenges to fight, violent, unpremeditated assaults, and even muggings on leaving the bar. If you hang out at such a bar, you are inviting elevated risks to your personal safety or you are going to "elevate someone else's risks," which may land you in jail. So if you don't want to get punched out or to punch someone else out, then set aside your penchant for adventure and stay away from bars with a well-justified reputation for drunken comportment, a ramped up dialogue of teasing, cursing and insults and a general atmosphere of interpersonal challenge, hostility and danger.

On some occasions, normally peaceful bars are transformed into high risk venues. Consider the example a situation in which it is known that rival football fans or acquaintances that hold a grudge against you or your friends are holding fort at the neighbourhood watering hole. To go is to literally anticipate a confrontation that could include broken bones and even more tragic outcomes. So why go? If you avoid the fight that is likely to ensue some will regard you as being afraid to fight. On the other hand, if you get into it, you might get your derriere kicked or you might hurt yourself and wind up in the "klink" with a serious assault charge. Who needs the grief? If you do, you might re-assign your status as a drinker and seriously consider an abstinence strategy. You should note that, ultimately, location is linked backward to motivation. Let's face it, if you go to a tough bar and you are not a sociologist or anthropologist doing a study, you expect to either witness or start a confrontation. To attend such bars is to literally "be asking for trouble."

ACTION STRATEGY 10: Set criteria for the limits you place on the quantity of alcohol you normally consume.

Establish a lifetime rule for your drinking limits. You have tapered down but where does that tapering finally settle. In Scene 9, you set your standard.

How much you drink places you at varying degrees of risk. As I indicated above, your BAL (blood alcohol level) will vary with a number of factors, including your size, gender and the tolerance you have developed over time, so the amount and time you need to drink before you are intoxicated will vary. KNOW YOUR LIMIT!!!

Before you drink, take a pause, and during the time you take for that pause, set specific rules and limits.

ACTION STRATEGY 11: Establish your personal, fail-safe criteria for that rare heavy drinking session.

Recognize that occasionally you might want to drink beyond your sobriety threshold. I certainly don't encourage it, ever, and, in fact, I have to say

Thinkin' Drinkin'

that the fewer times you over-indulge, the better. My best advice is that it is far better to find sober substitutes for satisfying the motivations that encourage a heavy drinking binge. I don't live on Mars, however, and I know that, on earth, sometimes individuals who are normally very sensible, moderate drinkers do decide to drop their typical restraint and engage in a heavy drinking session. If you do fall prey to such a temptation, here's some safety hints:

- ✓ Obviously, you shouldn't drink and drive (and make sure you have a safe, alternative way of getting home).

- ✓ Be with friends you trust and have a trustworthy designated driver who is capable of resisting those who change their mind about driving once their tight.

- ✓ If you can, do your heavy drinking at a home or at a hotel where you can stay overnight.

- ✓ If you do drink at home, ensure that you avoid causing any damage to the property of the homeowners. All drinkers should agree in advance to some basic rules regarding the avoidance of property damage—and make a commitment to jointly paying for any damage, with the greater share of repayment responsibility (say 30%-50% of the damage) to the individual actually, through carelessness or intention, actually caused the damage.

- ✓ If you are drinking in a public setting, do so in a safe venue. Avoid sports bars popular for their heavy drinking customers and, at all costs, avoid dangerous bars where gangs hang out or where assaults, fights and even the odd killing is part of the "character" of the establishment (And really do avoid these. Don't get drunkenly bold and adventurous and say, "Hey guys, let's go to 'Long John Silver's' and watch the trouble brewing.")

- ✓ Drink in numbers, with some of the mix remaining sober, and stick to your own crowd.

- ✓ Avoid confrontations and remember be aware of some tactics for defusing a situation.

- ✓ Unless someone is accompanied by a sober escort from the drinking group, don't let anyone who is impaired leave on their own—and don't you leave on your own.

- ✓ Find out any possible medical complications you and your drinking companions may have that are associated with interactions between booze and medications and between booze and various health conditions, including pregnancy—and don't drink – and especially don't drink heavily – if these apply to you and refuse to drink with or provide alcohol to anyone to whom these conditions apply.

- ✓ Try to have at least one or two individuals of intimidating size or with special skills to aid defusing confrontations on hand.

- ✓ Have a plan for restraining a friend who gets extremely drunk and belligerent.

I know this all sounds pretty serious but don't kid yourself; planning to get drunk is a very serious thing—and the risks involved are enormous. But don't get so drunk that you can't sustain the behaviour dictated by the guidelines of your plan.

ACTION STRATEGY 12: Plan out the basic rules for each (and every) drinking session you attend.

Planning your own participation in a drinking session, both as guest and host, is the focus of the next chapter **(Chapter 13)**.

ACTION STRATEGY 14: Establish compelling alternatives to frequent and heavy drinking

Finding pleasurable alternatives to drinking is the next **ACTION STRATEGY (i.e., #14)**, which is the focus of **Chapter 14** below.

Chapter 12

A Concrete Strategy for Sensibly (and Safely) Managing a Typical Drinking Session

---

Okay, so you've learned some common and effective tactics for preventing stinkin' drinkin' as part of your lifestyle. Now I'd like you to have another look at the matter, this time with a focus on handling a specific social drinking session—which is to say, *any* social drinking session...

Managing even a single drinking session can be a challenge, despite what you have developed as an overall strategy. Once you have begun such a session, your thinking patterns and emotions are soon affected by your mood, the setting, and the people, as well as the alcohol you are ingesting. There are many times that you feel very strongly that you want to "just stay for a one or two more drinks" and that can easily persist through several rounds. Unless you are very resolved, the goal moderating your drinking and controlling your behaviour can quickly slip away. So it is very important to have a clear approach to guiding yourself through the drinking session, from beginning to end.

So, remember, **FREEZE-FRAME** THE MOTIVATIONS BEHIND THE INTEREST IN A DRINKING SESSION AND BALANCE IT OFF WITH THE REASONS **NOT** TO DRINK. Don't go if an exceptional mood is going to take over or if you are overwhelmed by the pressure of friends—friends who you know will be pressing you to keep drinking to the point of drunkenness.

If you find yourself slipping into the beginnings of that initial euphoric confusion that having one too many ushers in, take it as a signal to quit—and scram. Get out of there. Immediately consider a satisfying alternative destination and activity. If possible, leave with an abstinent friend or acquaintance or take a cab home.

If you defy this logic *after* you know the old buzz is coming on, and you have decided to linger at the drinking session, at least switch to coffee, tea, water or pop, and stick with the option, perhaps alternating with a couple of additional drinks over several hours. Meanwhile, carry on with the spirit you wanted to achieve and just forget about the need to keep downing the beer, wine or cocktail. You really can learn to relax and enjoy an extended sitting by moderating the drinking aspect of your socializing. When you are in your psychic driver's seat, you can learn to use your own psychological skills to create a positive, good humoured mood or even an intense debate or exploration of feelings or ideas *without* relying on alcohol. Granted, it takes a little effort but you can do it. Yes, you really can. You really don't have to have that one beer and then run.

You should also consider the following specific tactics prior to the session, before that confusion occurs:

1. You should **limit your drinking session to a specific time** late in the day and set a minimum and maximum time for the session.—and *stop* **when you reach your limits**! Take full control over your drinking. Know your limits. Normally, drink only enough to feel a little relaxed, not to get tipsy and, except in the very rare, well managed circumstance, do not drink to the point of intoxication. Some people drink in order to get drunk. Others drink and then stop when they start becoming tipsy. It is wise to avoid drinking beyond your limit even if you feel no significant effects of the alcohol. *Remember* that alcohol takes some time before you can feel the effects.

2. **Drink slowly**. If you want to drink but don't want to get drunk before the party ends, don't drink like a fish drinking water. Slow down. If three bottles of beer is your limit, make the three bottles last until the end of the party and drink it over a sufficient length of time that you do not feel impaired. Insert some activity in between gulps. For example, take one gulp, then talk for thirty minutes or walk around and meet new people.

Drinking is actually fun and can facilitate social interaction—but only if it is done responsibly and moderately. You don't even need to drink if you don't want to.

3. **Keep track of how much you drink.** You might try moving an elastic band from finger to finger or putting bottle caps or swizzle sticks in your pocket to make sure you've got an accurate count of your drinks (and certainly don't ask for or pour "doubles" or "triples"). These are creative ways to keep count of how many drinks you have had. Sometimes, in the exchange of conversation, you'll find that time really flies and it is easy to lose sight of how many drinks we have had. Taking a count throughout the night is important if you want to make sure you don't go over your limit.

4. **Measure your drinks** if you are at a house party or other informal gathering. Don' simply pour directly from a bottle to your glass. There are few situations where it is easier to cheat on yourself.

5. **Set time limits** for your drinking. Setting a time limit for attending a party or going to the bar is often an effective approach to managing your drinking and maintaining your goal of sobriety. Knowing *when you start* and *how late you are going to stay* imposes an important discipline on your drinking.

6. **Set minimum times for each drink.** A "slow time" minimum can be set for each alcoholic beverage you consume—and even for the interval between each sip. Spacing drinks over longer periods of time makes it possible to have more control over the situation and the BAC level. It will also reduce the pain of next day's hangover. As a rule of thumb, don't have more than one drink per hour.

7. **Drink on a full stomach.** While drinking less alcohol is the only thing that will prevent you from getting drunk, if you don't want the alcohol to hit you quite as fast, make sure you eat a full meal. Whether you eat while you drink or before, drink on a full stomach. Make sure you have eaten a meal before you start drinking. Drinking on an empty stomach will make the alcohol work into your system faster and make you feel drunk faster. If you are looking to prevent hangovers, you might try eating an egg or two

and a small helping of sauerkraut before you drink. A lot of people think that works. It hasn't for me but it's worth a try.

8. **If you are drinking at a house or another private venue, don't buy large quantities of alcohol to take to the party.** Why? Simply because you might feel a little compelled to drink all that you have brought along. And avoid buying those boxes of wine that hide how much alcohol has been drained from its container. Those drinking vessels mask how much you have consumed and a little tipsiness can slide easily into serious drunkenness.

9. **Choose the least impairing beverages.** Some types of alcoholic beverage are stronger than others. For example, there is "light" beer and regular beer, with the measure distinguishing them being based on the relative concentration (percentage) of alcohol in the overall composition of the beverage. Different liquors and composite drinks like "coolers" also can have varying amounts of alcohol in them. Generally, the lower the alcohol content of a drink, the more of it you can drink before you become inebriated. Hard liquor usually has more alcohol content than beverages such as beer. There are also some drinks that seem to be less impairing than others and some that are less likely to leave a nasty hangover. You have to experiment with this to know what works for you. It is critical that you learn your drinking limits regarding different kinds of beverages. For example, you might find that you can drink up to three bottles of beer before starting to feel tipsy but, with tequila or whiskey, you can only take a shot or two. Be aware of the alcohol content.

10. **Keep yourself hydrated.** Drink lots of water—before the party, while drinking, and after the party. The water will help your body eliminate the alcohol faster.

11. **Alternate between drinks with alcohol and drinks lacking any alcohol content.** Rotate between alcoholic with non-alcoholic drinks, or keep one of each in front of you and alternate sips. If you want to avoid the promptings of those boring types who get anxious about other people not keeping up with them, alternate with an amber drink on ice, like ginger age or another common mix.

12. **Avoid Drinking Games.** Don't get into drinking games, like "chug-a-lug" contests. They ensure that you will get very drunk, sick and even dangerously intoxicated. In theory, such games are fun, but they're a lot more fun for the onlookers than for the drinker. If you think about it, the drinkers are actually getting shamefully exploited for the amusement of others. Why play the fool?

13. **If your motivation is sexual – like you are explicitly trying 'to get someone into bed' — then have some rules—and make sure you are sober when your intimacy arrives.** If you are going to drink and you know it might lead to bedding down with someone, then always have a condom with you, just in case. But beyond this little bit of practical advice, give some serious thought to the whole idea of drinking a few too many and having sex. Unfortunately, our drinking culture tends to encourage drinking as an excuse for sexual permissiveness. A drinking session is sometimes expected to create a shared state of mind that frees up potentially libidinal partners to go further in their sexual activity than they would in the absence of alcohol consumption. Unfortunately, there are no clear definitions or rules of sexual engagement. All too often, lubricated by a few drinks, unprotected sex occurs, with often grave results—the transmission of sexually transmitted disease or an unplanned pregnancy. Only moderate drinking should couple with sexual intimacy. The risks of heavy drinking and sex are huge.

14. **Know what you're doing before, during and after your drinking session—and stick to the plan.** Having several drinks is often treated as a "lubricant" to ease the transition from the tensions and anxieties of everyday sobriety to a feeling of being relaxed, looser, in a better mood, and more fun–all in preparation for events or activities that one is planning for. But what we are planning for also affects our mind set when and after we drink and it also affects how much we drink. Not having a set of clear, concrete goals that we are resolved to use as guides to our behaviour at a party is very foolish. It is this lack of clarity that leads to a lack of control and rational self-management, the kind of fuzzy thinking that leads us to regrettable behaviour like ragging on a friend, insulting and employer or teacher, sharing a confidence, and even to driving while impaired.

15. **Have a sensible and legal transportation plan.** Have access to a cab or a designated driver, bringing enough for gas and a tip for the driver and enough for the cab. In addition, if you live in a cold climate, *don't wander off in sub-zero temperature for home from a bar or a party* if you have had a few too many drinks—especially if you live a long way from the place you were drinking. Also, *don't wander the streets alone* after leaving a bar, especially if the bar or the walk home is in an area with a reputation for a lot of muggings and violence. *Bring enough cash to the place you will be drinking so that you can get a cab home.*

16. **Never drink just before or during the driving of a recreational vehicle or a boat.**

Basic Protocols for Hosting a Party in which Drinking is Allowed

Here are some basic protocols for hosting a party in which drinking is involved:

A host should always be sober (It's better not to drink at all). If you are in charge, have very little if anything to drink. Sobriety throughout the night is essential—and keep up a positive mood and a decisive point of view. If you become despondent and tired, the party can easily get out of your control. In a sense, you are the ringmaster in a circus of your own making.

Create an enjoyable and safe party atmosphere. As a host, you should do what you can to create a situation in which your guests not only enjoy themselves but in which their safety is assured. So think carefully, anticipate how the event can work smoothly and what to do if things get out of hand. A host should explicitly plan for and, during the party or event, monitor the safety of guests and the behaviour of individuals whose drinking or aggressive behaviour seems to be getting out of hand.

Create a sympathetic 'people plumbing' plan. Make sure everyone knows where the bathrooms are and have receptacles available if the bathrooms are closed and someone needs to, er . . . vomit.

Thinkin' Drinkin'

Don't assume alcohol is essential. You should learn to hold parties at which people don't assume that there will be alcohol consumed and are comfortable with that fact. If a get-together is assumed to be a drinking party, the drinking often becomes the focus of the event. If it is not known whether or not there will be drinking involved or if it is known that there probably isn't, then even if there are drinks available it is less likely that the party will evolve into a heavy drinking occasion or a truly wild party.

It takes a few successful parties to prove to friends that a drink-limited party can be a success but once it's done a few times, it can become quite a normal thing for you and your friends. You might even take the initiative and pro-actively facilitate the familiarization of friends with sober parties. Parties can involve attending sporting events and getting together for snacks and a movie after the event is over, playing cards or watching a Super Bowl game on TV. If you are living at your parent(s)' home and many of your friends drink, you have a ready-made excuse for bailing on the drinking aspect of a get-together: your parents won't allow drinking in the house. Once people get used to non-drinking parties, they don't expect it and the tension around policing the restriction typically disappears.

If you do want to allow drinking, the question becomes: How do you **optimize the safety of your guests** at the gathering?

Try to have a **sobriety monitor** in attendance at your party or be that person yourself. If it is not you, make sure the individual you ask to be a monitor can be relied upon and is "respected" physically by your group, while at the same time being a person who has a way with people and will do his best to avoid confrontations. If it is a very big party, you might consider paid security.

Try your best to **avoid the possibility of unfriendly 'party crashers.'** As you know, your apartment or your parents' home can get destroyed by people who show up that hardly know you, or know you and dislike you or have little respect for you. We've all heard about fights, stabbings, shootings, and even riots ignited by clashes with legitimate party-goers instigated by invited. Here's some suggestions for keeping the neandrathals away:

- ✓ Make sure to keep the address of your party known only to those you invite (if that is possible).

- ✓ If you see people showing up that look like they might make the party turn ugly, nicely explain to the uninvited guests that the party is a small, private affair–and do it immediately so the chances of the situation gradually escalating into something major are reduced.

- ✓ If you are pretty sure such an invitation to leave will merely result in conflict, then you might shut the party down with a legitimate, if contrived excuse. Ready-made excuses include the statement that your parents are coming home early or the guy in charge of the hall is complaining that there is too much noise and you have to take the party elsewhere.

An Ounce of Prevention is Worth a Pound of Cure

You can also **do some preventive things**. Consider the following:

Wisely select the people to be invited to the party. Make sure that the collection of people at the party are friendly, both with you and with each other. People who like each other are less likely to start throwing punches than people who don't.

If you can, ***invite guests of mixed of ages to the party.*** My experience is that sobriety and respectful behaviour are promoted by having a variety of types and ages of people. An all-male, young, single group of high testosterone party-goers tends to increase the probability of drunken behaviour and fights.

Dealing with Party Invaders

When an invasive threat is clearly anticipated, you have to act. If you think your party might get crashed by people intending to fight or vandalize your party venue, whether that is a residence or other party location, either cancel the party, lock the doors, and leave the residence, or have an alternative safety plan in place. Before the party, contact the police, advise them of the potential threat, and get the name of an officer you can call to ensure a quick response when it looks like things might get out of hand.

If you are intensely committed to avoiding police intervention or you are pretty sure you can't rely on their support, you might consider another approach. You might carefully anticipate the capacity for violence of your invasive crowd and check their intentions by having an even tougher bunch of guests on your side. If you choose the latter, strongly advise your "informal security" friends to only use force if all else fails. In any case, if you think there is an invasive threat, it is much wiser to cancel the party.

Physical Health and Safety Considerations

In addition to issues involving person-to-person confrontations that might lead to serious injuries, various things can happen that can result in health and safety risks, from falls, cut arteries from broken glasses, and crises associated with pre-existing health conditions. As a host, your safety plans should include:

Know all your local emergency numbers (911; ambulance; ER; police; fire fighters; emergency wards, etc.) and keep the list by your most accessible telephone.

Have a **first aid** kit available and, if you can, have someone on hand who knows first aid and CPR techniques.

Have a **plan for getting medical attention** for anyone who might go overboard or gets injured while drinking, such as hitting their head while falling down stairs. You should have contact numbers for ambulance companies that are closest to the venue where you are drinking, a doctor who might be willing to come to the house (although this is probably not possible), and ready access to a friend who might have first aid training.

Preventing Drinking and Driving

It need hardly be stated that it is also extremely important that you *make sure that no one at the party drinks and drives*. To avoid drunk driving on the part of party guests or having anyone at your party ride with a drunk driver:

- You should arrange for all your transportation needs in advance of a drinking occasion.

- You should select a reliable, designated driver who agrees that s/he will stay sober throughout the night or arrange for a cab or transportation by an older brother or sister, parent or relative who is reliable.

- You should tell people about the no-drinking-and-driving rule at the beginning of the party–and repeat it in a gentle, friendly but firm fashion a couple of more times throughout.

- Make sure those coming in the door are required to surrender their keys to the host in advance, who should keep them in a safe and secret place or with a designated driver (and monitor the designated driver to ensure that s/he isn't drinking).

- Arrange for the possibility of a sleep-over at the party site, if that is possible.

These precautions should ensure that the no driving and drinking rule is followed.

I know this listing of responsible actions makes the host role seem pretty onerous, but they should be taken seriously. The health and safety of your guests is at stake, as well as their enjoyment. **If you don't think you have the self-confidence to enforce these rules, then** *don't* **host the party.**

Chapter 13

Reinforcing Thinkin' Drinkin' By Finding More Satisfying Alternatives

To enable, reinforce and sustain a sensible drinking strategy, it is essential that you eliminate or at least substantially modify the ordinary routines and social circumstances that favour an immoderate habit of libation. In this chapter, I'm going to suggest some reasonable alternatives to frequent, heavy drinking, as well as drinking in binges that inevitably lead to intoxication. Some of it will seem trite, some inspiring guffaws, but in your more thoughtful moments, it may prove helpful.

Anticipating, carrying out and experiencing the outcomes of heavy drinking are all associated with various types of need satisfaction and enjoyment. These needs and types of enjoyment are really quite diverse: thirst-quenching – a little too much — on a hot day; getting together with good company at a bar; joining people at someone's house for a few drinks and a game of poker; and celebrating important events.

We enjoying the many things that we associate drinking with, including the delights of humour, the richness of debating ideas, the intensified intimacy of conversations and the pursuit of uninhibited sexual engagement. As I've gone to great lengths to point out, however, the risks associated with careless drinking are so very great that they virtually scream out for you to approach drinking with moderation in mind. It's hard to appreciate the importance of that statement at your age but someday it will strike you as astonishingly obvious.

You may not have thought about it but the fact is that all of those activities with which we routinely include alcoholic beverages can be done *without* the alcohol. I want you to think about that repeatedly as you proceed with this chapter.

For mobilizing activities that can function as healthy and enjoyable diversions from drinking as a pastime, consider the ideas below.

✓ **Acquire a taste for delicious, alternative beverages.**

While I have suggested strategies and tactics to establish moderate drinking as a drinking style, the same approach can be the key to a fundamentally healthy, enjoyable, and productive lifestyle in general. Reflection, setting interest priorities, establishing concrete life goals, and finding ways to reinforce their successful pursuit is a good formula for the management of any life.

Beginning with the thirst-quenching aspects of alcoholic drinks, let me help you explore some alternatives to stinkin' drinkin' that can be incorporated as good habits into your overall lifestyle.

Thirst-quenching is easy, of course. The fact is that the enjoyment of most alcoholic beverages is an acquired rather than immediate taste. For most part, it is the sweetness and flavouring that goes with an alcoholic drink that is the really enjoyable part of the tasting. Let's be honest, finding a better taste than even the best beers and ales is hardly a challenge and hard liquor, at least in any volume, is most often enjoyed because of the sweet, fruit-derived taste of the mix that goes with it. It is true that wines of various kinds can be delicious and the very expensive ones often are but in all honesty, so are various fruit drinks. The alcohol itself is mostly a mood-modifier, while only fine wines can truly be said to be a taste delight.

Be mindful that every restaurant and drinking establishment also serves non-alcoholic cocktails, various pop drinks, juices and an increasing range of delicious hot and cold coffee, tea, chocolate and fruit beverages.

✓ **Learn to socialize without the help of alcohol.**

Alcohol tends to accompany various types of socializing. In fact, many of us who have thought about the functions of alcohol consumption believe that as a society, North America has fundamentally failed young people by not producing a satisfactory approach to teaching the skills of enjoyable and effective socializing. All too often, drinking has been used as a lubricant to verbal engagement and a fortifier for those uncomfortable with easy and friendly patter and unskilled at striking up humorous or interesting conversation.

As teens and young adults, North Americans simply do not have a very rich and elaborate set of norms and protocols to guide our interactions with each other. Maybe it was the fact that, in creating societies on the North American continent, we were so intent on abandoning everything European that suggested differences of social class and privilege that we forgot to create our own, albeit improved and more egalitarian norms to guide our social comportment. If we are honest with ourselves, a visit to France, England or Italy will make you envious of the ease with which the routine of everyday discourse is filled with such rich, humorous and visibly expressive exchanges. By comparison, North American discourse tends to be pretty awkward. It's almost as if we have to reinvent how we talk to each other each time we have a conversation.

Hey folks, all is not lost. There is another way. You can learn the skills of conversation in particular and socializing on your own. There are books aplenty on communication skills, on how to build trust, on how to enrich the substance of your conversation, even on how to be humorous in a sarcastically-free fashion. But you don't learn all this from going to the bar.

Let's face it, drinking for North Americans is a substitute for conversational aptitude and other social skills that we lack; however, if you look hard enough, there is plenty of helpful advice around. You can identify people whose example models excellent socializing and conversational practices. You can also make a bit of a study about how to communicate effectively, how to interact socially in a satisfying, helpful, assertive and empathetic way.

Also by observing others, you can learn about and acquire positive leadership skills. Reading biographies of leaders in various realms can also be inspirational.

Finally, you can learn how to be a clever conversationalist and your can learn how to mingle and 'work a room,' as the saying goes.

Some attributes that will draw people to you and attract their return are outlined in the two column table below.

Table 3 Attributes that Attract Others

Engaging with others in a way that suggests that you regard them as having value as individuals.	Being sympathetic when you know someone needs help or more understanding when they are experiencing a crisis or significant disappointment.
Being authentic and genuine with people.	
Being polite (see the discussion below on civility)	Being empathetic, which means that you try to understand how you would feel if you found yourself in a difficult situation similar to one that another person confronts
Being welcoming and warm with people without being possessive of them or expecting something back that they haven't bargained for.	
	Maintaining confidences so that others believe they can talk to you privately and you won't broadcast what they shared with you to other people.
Being a good listener and showing that you are by trying to briefly summarize and paraphrase what someone else has said as a way of checking that you've understood what they are saying or that, if you don't, they are offered another chance to explain what they want you to understand.	
	Being accepting and respectful of other people's opinions, while clearly indicating your own opinion if you are asked.

✓ **All hail to Starbucks and such.**

It's hardly news that the coffee shop craze of recent decades competes favourably with bars, saloons and pubs for providing tasty beverages and social outlets. Most offer opportunities for plugging into the Internet, playing computer games or even doing a bit of word processing and various other kinds of homework. If a drinking establishment is the centre of your social universe, consider this alternative. You can actually have better conversations and be more comfortable sitting alone at a cool coffee shop than almost any drinking establishment—and you're less likely to have a headache after you leave.

- ✓ **Find more thrilling alternatives.**

For some people, heavy drinking is associated with thrill-seeking. Going out for a drink can lead to all kinds of fun, to parties, to sex, to getting the courage to confront an enemy. Yet if you think about it, that's a pretty lame way of truly seeking an adventurous, thrilling afternoon or evening. Why not do the real thing, without the fortification of duller thinking and senses?

People who are truly thrill seekers get involved in adrenalin-pumping activities like sky-diving, bunji jumping, rock-climbing, white water rafting, horseback riding, motocross racing, hiking or canoeing in remote areas, or one of the martial arts. Those people find huge excitement confronting danger, exploring unknown terrain and testing their personal courage and problem-solving skills. If you have a thrill-seeking personality – and some psychological research strongly suggests that there is such a thing – then you might try these alternatives rather than going on wild and crazy drunks. The thrill is surely far more spine-tingling and memorable. Adrenalin rushes of this intensity are not everybody's thing, of course (including mine), although the odd roller coaster ride or parachute jump can surely recharge one's batteries.

> **People who are truly thrill seekers get involved in adrenalin-pumping activities like sky-diving, bunji jumping, etc. By comparison, getting drunk is pretty lame.**

For most of you, thrills can be sought in far safer individual and team sports and endurance activities. Taking one of those activities on as a major challenge can become a central and healthier part of your lifestyle—and one that is hardly bolstered by, or even compatible with, heavy drinking.

But whether it's long-distance running or competitive amateur tennis, ball hockey, roller-blading, getting engaged in a regular, high intensity physical activity can prove immensely satisfying. Inadvertently, it also tends to push too much drinking off your usual agenda of enjoyable things to do.

✓ **Take up an ordinary hobby—and get into it with a passion.**

I know it sounds a little hokey, at least for some of you, but finding alternatives to drinking that are thoroughly enjoyable and consuming – in other words, getting a hobby – is a great alternative to frequent and heavy drinking. Some of you will already be into hobbies of various kinds but if you're not, think of all the possibilities.

Of course there are the video games and various Internet-related hobbies—and I'm sure most of you will know about them.

I had a friend in my teens who took up customizing cars with an older friend when he was sixteen. To say the least, he was a wild and crazy drinker. His hobby became his passion, however, eventually turning into *both* a business and a lifetime hobby and his drinking faded from his life. No time for it.

You might consider the list of hobbies on the next page – and many still are – very popular, then you might circle your favourites as part of your thinkin' drinkin' or abstinence strategy.

Some Popular Hobbies to Consider			
Singing or playing an instrument in a rock group	Writing short stories or poetry	Stamp collecting	Weight-lifting
Starting a garage band	Joining a drama club	Learning about antiques	Motocross racing
Join a rap group	Joining a track and field club	Learning to paint—and painting	Dirt biking

Thinkin' Drinkin'

Some Popular Hobbies to Consider			
Learning to play a musical instrument	Getting involved with some form of dance—ethnic, hip-hop, ballroom, ballet, jazz, lyrical, etc.	Learning to sculpt—and sculpting	Ski-dooing (in the summer, watercraft riding)
Joining an athletic team in a sport you enjoy	Restoring or customizing cars	Learning wood-carving—and doing it.	Sail boating (or sail-boarding)
Spending more time playing informal pick-up sports	Learning about electronics by assisting a small business owner	Drawing	Skiing or snowboarding in the winter
Go camping or fishing with friends	Fishing	Wood-working and carpentry	Marathon running
Learn to be a DJ—and become one, part-time	Biking	Body-building	Playing pool
Swimming and diving	Yoga or Pilates	Martial arts	Tai-chi
Tennis	Speed skating	Bowling	Coaching
Table tennis	Scrabble or other Board games	Bridge or other card games	Badminton
Knitting and/or sewing	Designing and making clothes	Ethnic or multi-national cooking and/or baking	Jewellery making
Others (that you want to add): Add in space to the right			

✓ **Develop friendships anchored in sobriety.**

I know I'm repeating myself a little here but the point is so important that you should indulge me—and I'm expanding it a bit. In earlier parts of the book, I made the point that it is rare that real, lasting friendships are forged through drinking sessions. Yet often we use gatherings at the bar or drinking at parties as a means of creating the semblance of a meaningful social life and expression of group bonding. Admit it, that liquid camaraderie is a poor substitute for the friendships forged and maintained while sober. Sober relationships involve helping each other out with moving to a new apartment, doing work to upgrade a house to make it more habitable, engaging in sporting activities or evening card sessions together, and making sure each other is safe at dances or major events. A real friendship is constituted of a minimum of two people who can rely on each other for support and as a listening ear, confidant and helping hand when things aren't going so well. A friendship circle is a bunch of people bound by activities and commitments of this kind that overlap with each other.

Work at developing some very close and strong primary friendships and a pretty good second flight of friends—and do so with those who are sensible drinkers or abstainers. You don't need the complications posed by stinkin' drinkers when you're trying to get your act together. Once you're on pretty solid ground in that department, however, you will probably find yourself able to truly lend an effective helping hand to friends who are themselves struggling with the issue.

Finally, avoid dependent relationships, with you as either the dominant, always in control one, or as a submissive person, always yielding to the decisions of others. Asymmetrical relationships are fraught with all kinds of frustrating social and psychological dynamics and tend to encourage a two-way course of emotional abuse.

✓ **Master the arts of intimacy and love.**

Heavy drinking and bizarre behaviour while drinking is extremely destructive for caring, loving relationships, setting complications in motion that tax and tarnish the innocence and beauty of tender, mutual kindness and support. Unfortunately, too many writers, playwrights, scriptwriters and poets have celebrated drinking as a major element in the expression of romantic love. The 'b.s' that so many drinkers use to describe their intimacies and sexual experiences add layer upon layer to the illusion that love, good sex and drinking are positively related. The fact of the matter is rather that heavy drinking is far more likely to lead to lies, carelessness, insensitivity, bullying and abuse than to the truly joyful possibilities of profound intimacy or thrilling sex.

Think about yourself as a sensitive and carrying human being. If you do, you'll find that relationships are all about caring attitudes, acquired knowledge of your partner, thoughtfulness and practical, mutually supportive work rather than magic bullets of indulgence, typically associated with binges of alcohol or drugs.

Enjoying the detail of intimacy and love is heightened by a clear mind. Alcohol numbs the experience of sex, undermines the skills of love-making and encourages selfish sex. Sobriety makes possible the caring, clear-mindedness, and special sensitivity to the needs of others that is required to master sexual intimacy. If you want to take your partner's breath away, you will find that a clear and heightened consciousness rather than a central nervous system depressant (which is what ethanol is) will be a far better bet.

✓ **Overcome your social 'neediness' by learning to enjoy solitude.**

Drinking is often used to fill the void of a lingering loneliness. Not a good plan for the lonely. Learning to get closer to more people and develop intimacies, a few very close friends and a network of good if not intimate friends is one pro-active solution that beats drinking on many fronts. There is also another front that you should never forget.

It has been said that, ultimately, each of us is our own best friend. At least if we don't drink stupidly, use drugs stupidly and if we have a clear and purposeful sense of our own lives and we are true to that purpose, then, as individuals, we are truly our own most truly trustworthy of soul. We are even a better friend to ourselves than our fathers, our brothers, our sisters and our lovers could possibly be. We are our own best father, our own best mother and our most loyal and concerned supporter. We are also our best own big brother or sister when it comes to calculating our own best interests and deciding what we can best do for other people. We know what we are personally most skilled at doing, most interested in doing, and what we most seriously believe in. As individuals we are also the only person on earth who truly knows what we best enjoy.

You know where I'm going with this.

Neither are we all social butterflies nor are all social butterflies always in need of the company of other people. People can be taxing and some people are almost nothing but taxing, so they can be very high maintenance. Sometimes we need relief from them: time out from the buttons other people push on us; time away from the crew in the hood, the team, the classroom or office politics; time away from intimates who expect too much of us, who are trying to control or manipulate us; respite from others whose dependence on us is exhausting.

For most of you, drinking is probably a social endeavour. You do it as a part of social occasions, to make social occasions happen, or to modify your mood so that, presumably, you can socialize with more confidence and in a more relaxed way. I've discussed other alternatives to the persuasive, heavy drinking situation characteristic of so many social drinking situations. An alternative and admittedly obvious alternative is to avoid stinkin' drinkin' by learning to spend more of those otherwise social drinking occasions by ourselves.

One reason to spend time away from others is that there is much to do alone, and what there is to do alone is increasing by the day. Think about it. There is reading, doing yoga, becoming a long-distance runner, getting involved in Iron Man competitions, working out at a gym spontaneously on your own schedule, taking in movies or downloading them from *Netflix*. I need hardly remind you of video games that can be played alone or the games that can be played on the computer. And of course, there are also a freight load full of options for solo hobbies, from writing and learning and playing a musical instrument through building architectural models or models of ships, airplanes, robots and collecting things, from stamps to bugs to baseball cards or even the beginnings of an antique car, furniture or art collection (Don't laugh, some collectors who are now millionaires had their raw beginnings in their mid-teens).

Doing things alone can also involve more profound kinds of experiences, such as meditation, thoughtful walks and jogging, and lengthy bouts of self-examination.

Solitude should not be considered a "spell of loneliness" but, rather, a time for doing a full range of things, from just enjoying yourself in a situation where you don't have to worry about the needs of other people to profound contemplation: a time to get in touch with your deepest emotions and thoughts. It is not about suffering through an evening with your own company but taking the time to befriend yourself and taking some time to think about how best we want to approach other people, upcoming challenges and even re-evaluating our life goals—and for considering the best alternatives for trying to achieve them.

✓ **Don't be self-centred. Get off your butt and help the environment, the community and the less advantaged.**

The idea is hardly rare that giving to your community has value, both to the community *and* you. In other words, altruistic work – that $60 word intentionally doing things of benefit to others — should not be considered charity but as mutually rewarding activity As the addictions specialist Stanton Peele has written, "Being a part of something larger than yourself—making contributions to other people's lives—provides you with the life purpose and meaning that will sustain you through times of trouble" (*7 Tools to Beat Addiction*, 2004).

Peele argues that helping others and making a contribution to your community "reduces the impulse to be addicted" and, I would add, it also reduces the impulse to engage in frequent, binge drinking. As Peele argues, being busy with the challenges of helping

> **The answer to shifting away from bad habits like heavy drinking is to tap into your social conscience, to make yourself busy with important work... In the process, a lot of your personal obsessions and everyday worries simply shrink into their true status of trivia and gradually disappear entirely from your mental radar screen.**

others in the community crowds out the impulse to addiction or binge drinking. What happens is that you displace your personal worries and self-absorption with concerns for and actions taken to help others.

Despite what a trainload full of commercial advertising communicated in every media would like you to believe, neither the hot new car, dressing according to the latest fashion, having the best sports equipment and the most frequent and luxurious vacations, nor a life of drink-addled club visits, parties and hot dates, are the real keys to profound satisfaction, pride and happiness. The thing that truly brings you self-satisfaction is serving a purpose bigger than yourself, by which I mean giving much of what you've got to helping to create a better family, friendship network, school, neighbourhood, community, state or province, nation or world.

The answer to shifting away from bad habits like heavy drinking is to tap into your social conscience, to make yourself busy with important work that boosts your self-esteem. In the process, a lot of the personal obsessions and worries about yourself – from the clothes you are wearing through the wheels you drive to your adolescent case of acne – shrink into triviality. When you are raising money for Haiti relief, working as a "big brother" or "big sister" to younger people with needs, volunteering in the organization of the Special Olympics, or working on a green program that encourages students to drive to campus on bikes rather than cars, a lot of your personal troubles start to seem pretty minor. Not only is your self-esteem enhanced in the process, you actually come to reframe your perspective on the world. This emerges as you refocus from your own needs on to those of other people or the environment. In the process, your own "issues" tend to wither and fade away.

As lifestyle writer Pam Grout advocates in her book, *Living Big* (2001), "Grow up and get over yourself … When we really become big enough to serve, to give it all away with no expectation, our sense of personal power, our peace of mind, and our ability to love and trust takes giant steps."

Chapter 14

Afterward

In this book I champion maturity of thought and action when it comes to drinking—and what I am advocating can apply to any other significant, pleasurable but potentially high risk behaviour.

In my opinion, responsibility is the prerequisite, the driving force behind, genuine maturity. In turn, responsibility is based on discipline; it involves a sustained commitment to a set of rules to which one consciously ascribes.

When you're a kid, for the most part, you have to march to the dictates of parents, sometimes even older siblings, as well as various authority figures, such as teachers, principals, ministers and priests, neighbourhood centre coordinators, store proprietors and, sometimes, police officers. The result is that most of the time you simply have to "do what you're told," as the saying goes.

In your childhood, doing what others tell you to do is often essential to your protection and nurture, so, most of the time, doing what adults tell isn't really so awful. Yet at some point, you have to be weaned from that almost automatic obedience. You will want to be freed up to march to your own orders and your own beat—and that is very liberating: in general, it is something which, at some point, you will desperately want. To obtain that sweet mind and social

> **Maturity brings responsibility and responsibility brings many burdens. Responsible drinking is in fact a marker of maturity; it is a characteristic of an individual who doesn't let alien ideas or other people do her thinking for her (or him).**

space called *independence*, much of the irresponsibility of being a kid has to be set aside. In short, you have to become mature.

Maturity is a blessing unto itself. It offers the opportunity for personal empowerment: the power to control far more of your life than you were able to as a child or as a young teen. You will quickly find that, despite its advantages, maturity itself is a burdensome thing, often *very* burdensome.

Being personally empowered is about deciding what you believe in and figuring out how to make sure that you, not anybody else, but you, are the person in charge of your own actions. It involves consistently enacting behavioural patterns that you believe in.

In short, maturation itself is about growing up in a good way, as a strong person, a person with character, someone who you would trust and admire if you were someone else.

When we are personally empowered, we make most of the important decisions in our lives according to what we believe in. In other words, our choices to act are made in a manner that is quite different than simply acting on impulse or responding to the heat of the moment, circumstance, or the persuasion of others.

Maturity doesn't mean that you can operate in full independence of the will of others and the rules of family, community and society. In fact, what it really means is that you have become consciously *interdependent*. You have made a choice to figure out and act upon how *you* want to co-operate with and, at times, resist and dissent from the ideas and actions of others; it is not adopting a stance that always insists you get your own way, that old "My way or the highway" approach.

> Thinkin' drinkin' is about empowerment in a general sense. It is about learning to exert your personal power in relation to drinking and, by extension, over all your basic life choices.

I strongly believe that, ultimately, to live well and to have a good measure of happiness on life's journey, we – all of us, and that means you — must accept that we are responsible for our own choices–and that responsibility expands enormously when we become adults.

Even when we submit to the pressures of the moment or the will of others you are making choices of a sort. I call them "half choices" because we really don't put much into them except ultimately, agreeing to go with the immediate flow.

Much of what we do in our lives is, in fact, based on half-choices but, in some instances, half-choices are very dangerous because they don't give us the time to apply our best thinking to the decisions at hand and the actions we take.

The adolescent years and the early twenties are the bridging years, the time that the dependency of a child on adult decisions and guidance gradually but rather quickly fades. In its place new responsibilities and significantly greater rights and authorities are gained.

To become fully responsible for your choices, you must identify and examine the lifestyle decisions you typically make, as well as the reasoning behind them, and then carefully consider your options. You almost always do have options, despite the fact that it is, at times, very hard to see more than one choice before you. Adolescence is an excellent place to begin.

After identifying your options, it is important to compare the likely outcomes of the choices to what you really believe in; in other words, it is important to determine *if* the anticipated outcomes fit with your values and our goals in life.

It has been my premise in writing this book that the key to a good life is personal empowerment, the power to make the choices that best support your values and goals in life—and then to develop the resolve to enact the principles and strategies that enable you to achieve what you are seeking on our personal life journey.

Making a choice about how you manage your alcohol consumption is one of the important choices you will have to make.

I hope you have been able to use the material in this book to become the permanent master of your own drinking (or non-drinking) choices. If you have, CONGRATULATIONS!

For those of you who have used the material to help you achieve abstinence, your courage and resolve is to not only be commended but celebrated. Both addicted alcohol use and problem drinking accompanied by bizarre behaviour pose extreme challenges for the afflicted individual. Those who overcome such behaviour do a great service to themselves and others; however, it should also be acknowledged that overcoming them is no easy feat and success is a real achievement. Most human behaviour satisfies some need, no matter how ineffective it may be in a comparative sense. So changing a behaviour that has served us by meeting an important need is a real challenge. Be proud of your accomplishment.

Also CONGRATULATIONS to those of you who have not had special problems with drinking but you have recognized the inherent risks in thoughtless drinking and have therefore developed a commitment to a sensible drinking strategy as a permanent feature of your personal lifestyle. This is also is a huge accomplishment, even though it comes to seem very natural, very easy, as the months and years go by. More than many decisions you will have to make in your life, adopting a thinkin' drinkin' stance puts you squarely in the winner's column of any useful quality of life measure.

I strongly encourage all of you to continue your success and, to this end, I hope that you find it useful to renew your resolve by referring back, on occasion, to the material I've provided you, as well as many of the references that are cited at the back of the book.

If You Need Additional Support, Be Choosy

For those of you have tried but failed to establish a thinkin' drinkin' or thinkin'-not-drinkin' lifestyle, and drinking is still a troubling issue in your life, I strongly advise you to try and try again. In that process, I suggest that you revisit the contents of this book and that you also seek the services of a professional Counsellor and, if possible, a self-help group.

Hopefully, you will be able to find the kind of supportive counselling you need. In my opinion, you should look for an individual Counsellor that understands that your challenges can best be met with self-directed strategies based in practical cognitive and social skills. You might have to shop around a bit to find that kind of help but surely it's worth the effort.

If you're looking for a support group, find one that provides you with various kinds of interpersonal encouragement for your efforts but also one that treats *you* as the master, the director, the central protagonist, of your personal drama, your very own, individual struggle with alcohol problems. If the group seems to encourage dependency or the perception that the answer lies in external sources, walk, no run, away to find another group. If there isn't one, then just find some help from a Counsellor, parents, siblings or friends you trust who recognize that, ultimately, you must modify your own thoughts and behaviour before you overcome the problem.

In closing this narrative, let me say that I would really appreciate hearing from you. Your stories would be very helpful in preparing an update in a new edition that might be published in the future, depending on the demand, of course. Even if you have failed in your efforts to become a *thinkin' drinker or thinkin' non-drinker* to date, I still want to hear your stories. Maybe I can give you some suggestions and include your challenges and future successes in subsequent versions of the book.

You can contact me by e-mail at: rthatcher@sasktel.net.

References

Addictions Research Foundation. *The Costs of Substance Abuse in Canada, 2002.* Toronto: Centre for Addiction and Mental Health (CAMH). 2002.

Alcohol & Anxiety Medication | eHow.com http://www.ehow.com/about_5456598_alcohol-anxiety-medication.html#ixzz1CG6DWBc2

American Psychiatric Association. Diagnostic and Statistical Manual of Mental Disorders (4th Edition) – referred to colloquially as 'DSM-IV.' Published in 1994. The 5the edition will soon be available.

Bayer, Lee. *Getting Control: Overcoming Your Obsessions and Compulsions.* New York: Penguin (A Plume Book). 1992.

Brands, Bruna (Ed.), with Associate Editors Meldon Kahan, Peter Selby, and Lynn Wilson, *Management of Alcohol, Tobacco and Other Drug Problems.* 3rd Edition. Toronto: Addiction Research Foundation (ARF), a division of the Centre for Addiction and Mental Health. 2000.

Blum, Kenneth and Helga Topel. "Opioid Peptides and Alcoholism: Genetic Deficiency and Chemical Management." *Functional Neurology* 1 (1986): 71-83.

Chatterji, Pinka and Jeffrey DeSimone. *High School Alcohol and Young Adult Labour Market Outcomes.* National Bureau of Economic Research. 2007.

Cloninger, Robert C., "Genetic and Environmental Factors in the Development of Alcoholism," *Journal of Psychiatric Treatment and Evaluation* 5 (1983): 487-96.

Cloninger, Robert C.; Soren Sigvardsson; and Michael Bohman, "Childhood Personality Predicts Alcohol Abuse in Young Adults," *Alcoholism: Clinical and Experimental Research* 5 (4, 1988): 494-505.

Center for Science in the Public Interest. "Representative Kennedy Lauded for 6-pack Approach to Alcohol Advertising." Press Release. May 16, 1996.

Centre for Addiction and Mental Health (CAMH). *The Avoidable Costs of Alcohol Abuse in* Canada. Prepared by Dr. Jurgen Rehm. 2002.Economic Burden of Alcohol Abuse in Canada. Costs each Canadian $463 per year.

Coleman, James, *The Adolescent Society*. New York: The Free Press. 1961.

Collins, Michael A.; Edward J. Neafsey; Kenneth J. Mukami; Mary O. Gray; Dale A. Parks; Dipak K. Das; and Ro;nald J. Korthuis. "Alcohol in Moderation, Cardioprotection and Neurolprotection: Epidemiological Considerations and mechanistic Studies." *Alcoholism: Clinical and Experimental Research*. Feb., 2009, Vol. 33, Issue 2. Pp. 206-219.

Cudney, Milton R., and Robert E. Hardy, *Self-Defeating Behaviours: Free Yourself from the Habits, Compulsions and Feelings that Hold You Back*. New York: Harper-Collins.1991.

Dorsman, Jerry. *How to Quit Drinking without AA. A Complete Self-Help Guide*. (2nd Revised edition). New York: Three Rivers Press. 1997.

Doweiko, Harold F. *Concepts of Chemical Dependency* (2nd edition). Pacific Grove, California: Brooks-Cole Publishing Co. 1993.

Duhachek, Adam and Nidhi Agrawal "Emotional Compatibility and the Effectiveness of Anti-Drinking Messages: A Defensive Processing Perspective on Shame and Guilt" will be published in a forthcoming in *the Journal of Marketing Research*.

Ferguson, Jack. "Eskimos in Satellite Society." In J.L. Elliott (ed.), *Native Peoples*, Scarborough: Prentice-Hall. 1971.

Fleeman, William. *The Pathways to Sobriety Workbook*. Alameda California: Hunter House. 2004.

Fletcher, Anne M. *Sober for Good*. New York and Boston: Houghton-Mifflin. 2001.

Campus Voice, pp. 61-63. 1985.

Friedman, Nancy. "Anatomy of a Drink," *Campus Voice*, pp. 61-63. 1985.

Goldstein, Dora, *Pharmacology of Alcohol* (New York: Oxford University Press, 1983).

Goleman, Daniel. *Emotional Intelligence. Why it Can Matter More than IQ*. New York: Bantam Books, 1995.

Goodwin, Donald W. "Alcohol Problems in Adoptees Raised Apart from Alcoholic Biological Parents," *Journal of Psychiatric Treatment and Evaluation* 5 (1973): 283-84.

Greenblatt, JC., "Patterns of Alcohol Use Among Adolescents and Associations with Emotional and Behavioural Problems," U.S. Department of Health and Human Services, Substance Abuse and Mental Health Services Administration, March 2000.

Grimes, William. *Straight Up or On the Rocks: A Cultural History of American Drink*. New York: Simon and Schuster, 1993.

Haring, Raymond H. *Shattering Myths & Mysteries of Alcohol*. Sacramento, California: HealthSpan Communications. 1998.

Heath, Dwight. "Prohibition and Post-Repeal Drinking Patterns Among the Navaho." *Quarterly Journal of Studies on Alcohol*. Vol. 25, No. 1. 1964.

Hyde, Margaret O. And John F. Setaro, MD. *Alcohol 101: An Overview for Teens*. Brookfield, Connecticut: Twenty-First Century Books. 1999.

Levinthal, Charles F. *Drugs, Behaviour, and Modern Society* (3rd Edition). Boston: Allyn and Bacon. 2002.

Levy, D.T.; T.R. Miller and K.C. Cox, *Costs of Underage Drinking*. Washingtgon, DC: Office of Juvenile Justice and Delinquency Prevention.

Li, Ting Kai et al, Rodent Lines Selected for Factors Affecting Alcohol Consumption," *Alcohol and Alcoholism,"* (Supp 1, 1987): 91-96.

MacAndrew, Craig and Robert B. Edgerton, *Drunken Comportment.* Chicago: Aldine. 1969.

McClearn, G.E.; R.A. Deitrich; and V.G. Erwin (eds.), *Development of Animal Models as Pharmacogenetic Tools* (USDHHS-NIAAA Research Monograph, No. 6, Washington, D.C., 1981. Pp. 171-181.

Miller, Geri. *Learning the Language of Addiction Counseling.* 2nd edition. Hoboken, New Jersey: John Wiley & Sons.

Miller, William R. And Ricardo F. Munoz, *Controlling Your Drinking: Tools to Make Moderation Work For You.* New York and London: The Guilford Press. 2005.

Mitchell, Hayley R. *Teen Alcoholism.* San Diego: Lucent Books. 1998.

Muisener, Philip A. *Understanding and Treating Adolescent Substance Abuse.* Thousand Oaks, California: Sage Publications. 1994.

Myers, Judy, with Maribeth Mellin. *Staying Sober.* New York: Condon Books. 1987.

National Institute on Alcohol and Alcoholism. *Alcohol Alert: Alcohol Metabolism.* No. 35. Bethesda, MD. 1997.

National Institute on Alcohol Abuse and Alcoholism (NIAAA) *Problem Drinker Data from Alcohol Cost Calculator for Business, 2005: Ensuring Solutions to Alcohol Problems.* George Washington University Medical Centre. 2005

National Institute on Alcohol Abuse and Alcoholism (NIAAA). "Alcohol and Women: An Overview," in *Tenth Special Report to Congress on Alcohol,* pp. 253-257. Rockville, MD: Geri Miller, Author.

National Institute on Alcohol Abuse and Alcoholism (NIAAA). *Tenth Special Report to the U.S. Congress on Alcohol and Health: Highlights from Current Research, From the Secretary of the U.S. Health and Human Services,*

Public Health Service, National Institute of Health, National Institute on Alcohol Abuse and Alcoholism. Rockville, MD.: NIAA. 2000.

National Institutes of Health (NIH). "Alcohol: What You Don't Know Can Harm You." NIH Publication No. 99-4323. Bethesdam Md.:NIH.

National Institute on Drug Abuse. "Gender Matters in Drug Abuse." *NIDA Notes*. 13, pp. 59-60.

National Institutes of Health, Underage Drinking, *Alcohol Alert*, Number 67, January 200.

National Institute on Alcohol Abuse and Alcoholism (NIAAA). *Tenth Special Report to the United States Congress on Alcohol and Health: Highlights from Current Research, From the Secretary of Health and Human Services, Public Health Service, National Institute of Health, National Institute on Alcohol and Alcoholism*. Rockville, Md.: NIAAA. 2000.

National Institutes of Health (NIH). "Alcohol: What You Don't Know Can Harm You." NIH Publication No. 99-4323. Bethesdam Md.:NIH.

National Institute on Alcohol Abuse and Alcoholism (NIAAA) *Problem Drinker Data from Alcohol Cost Calculator for Business, 2005: Ensuring Solutions to Alcohol Problems*. George Washington University Medical Centre. 2005

Parada, Maria; Montserrat Corral; Francisco Caamano-Ismano; Nayara Moto; Alberto Crego; Socorro Rodriguez Holguin; Fernanco Cadveira. 'Binge Drinking and Declarative Memory in University Students.' *Alcoholism: Clinical and Experimental Research*. August, 2011.

Peele, Stanton, and Archie Brodsky, *The Truth About Addictions and Recovery*: *The Life Process Program for Outgrowing Destructive Habits*. New York: Simon and Schuster. 1991.

Peele, Stanton. *7 Tools to Beat Addictions*. New York: Three Rivers Press. 2004.

Peele, Stanton. "The Conflict between Public Health Goals and the Temperance Mentality." *American Journal of Public Health.* 1993; 83: 805-810.

Peele, Stanton and Archie Brodsky, "The Antidote to Alcohol Abuse: Sensible Drinking Messages." See *The Stanton Peele Website.*

Peters, Bethany L. And Edward P. Stringham. *No Booze?: You May Lose.* The Reason Foundation, 2006 (A report on the Reason Foundation website, September, 2006. The formal study is reported in the *Journal of Labour Research.*

Prochaska, J.O.; C.C. DiClemente; and J.C. Norcross. "In Search of How People Change: Applications to Addictive Behaviour." *American Psychologist,* 47, 1102-1114.

Rehm, J.; D. Beliunas; S. Brochu; B. Fischer; W. Gnam; J. Patra; S. Popova; A. Sarnocinska-Hart; and B. Taylor, in collaboration with E. Adlaf; M. Recel; and E. Single. *The Costs of Substance Abuse in Canada: 2002.* Ottawa, Ontario: Canadian Centre for Substance Abuse. 2002.

Rohner, Ronald P. And Evelyn C. Rohner. *The Kwakiutl Indians of British Columbia.* New York: Holt, Rinehart and Winston. 1970.

Rosenbaum, Dennis P., Ph.D. and Gordon S. Hanson, Ph.D., April 6, 1998. *Assessing the Effects of School-Based Drug Education: A Six-Year Multi-Level Analysis of Project.*

Rotgers, Frederick; Marc F. Kern; and Rudy Hoeltzel. *Responsible Drinking: A Moderation Management Approach for Problem Drinkers.* Oakland, California: New Harbinger Publications. 2002.

Sanchez-Craig, M., et al. "Empirically Based Guidelines for Moderate Drinking: 1-year Results from Three Studies with Problem Drinkers. *American Journal of Public Health* 85: 823-828.

Sanchez-Craig, M. *Drinkwise: How to Quit Drinking or Cut Down.* 2nd ed. Toronto: Addiction Research Foundation. 1993.

Sobell, Linda and Mark Sobell, *Problem Drinkers: Guided Self-Change Treatment.* New York: Guilford Press. 1993.

Smith, G. Et al. "Fatal Non-traffic Injuries Involving Alcohol: A Meta-Analysis." *Annals of Emergency Medicine*. 33:699-702. 1999

Stevens, Patricia and Robert L. Smith. *Substance Abuse Counseling: Theory and Practice*. 3rd edition. Upper Saddle River, New Jersey: Pearson-Merrill (Prentice-Hall).

Substance Abuse and Mental Health Services Administration. *The National Household Survey on Drug Abuse*. 2001.

Tabakoff, Boris et al, "Differences in Platelet Enzyme Activity between Alcoholics and Non-Alcoholics," *New England Journal of Medicine*. 313 (1988): 134-39.

Thatcher, Richard. *Fighting Firewater Fictions: Moving Beyond the Disease Model of Alcoholism in First Nations*. Toronto: University of Toronto Press. 2004.

U.S. Department of Justice, *Alcohol and Crime: An Analysis of National Data on the Prevalence of Alcohol Involvement in Crime*. 1998.

U.S. Department of Transportation, *Traffic Safety Facts 2000*. Washington, D.C.: National Center for Statistics and Analysis, DOT HS 809 323.

Vaillant, George. *The Natural History of Alcoholism: Causes, Patterns, and Paths to Recovery*. Cambridge: Harvard University Press. 1983.

Valee, Bert L. "Alcohol in the Western World." *Scientific American*. June, 1998.

Wallace, John. "A Biopsychosocial Model of Alcoholism." *Social Casework: The Journal of Contemporary Social Work* Volume 70, 6: June, 1989: 325-332.

Walters, G.D. "Behavioural Self-Control Training for Problem Drinkers: A Meta-Analysis of Randomized Control Studies." *Behaviour Therapy*. 31:135-149.

Wells, S. et al. "Alcohol-related Aggression in the General Population." *Journal of Studies on Alcohol*. 61(4): 626-632.

Appendix

There are hundreds of screening tests for alcohol problems available, including some elaborate ones with up to 150 questions, short screening tests with only a few questions have been developed to encourage diagnosis in primary and emergency health-care situations.

The shorter tests may not be as accurate or sensitive as the longer ones, but they serve well to screen harmful drinking or alcohol dependence which can be followed up with further in-depth assessment using the more elaborate tests.

The CAGE Test

One of the oldest and most popular self-screening tools for alcohol abuse is the CAGE test, which is a short, four-question test that diagnoses alcohol problems over a lifetime.

C - Have you ever felt you should **cut down** on your drinking?

A- Have people **annoyed** you by criticizing your drinking?

G - Have you ever felt bad or **guilty** about your drinking?

E - **Eye opener**: Have you ever had a drink first thing in the morning to steady your nerves or to get rid of a hangover?

Because denial usually accompanies alcohol abuse problems, the CAGE test, like most alcohol screening tests, asks questions about problems associated with drinking rather than the amount of alcohol consumed. Two "yes" answers to the CAGE test indicates that you *currently* have problems with alcohol that you should address. It does not mean that you are an alcoholic, but it does mean that you should pursue further testing with the help of a trained professional.

The disadvantage of the CAGE test is that it is most accurate for white, middle-aged men and not very accurate for identifying alcohol abuse in older people, white women, and African and Mexican Americans.

The T-ACE Test

The T-ACE test is also only four questions, including three found on the CAGE test, but it has proved to be more accurate in diagnosing alcohol problems in both men and women.

The T-ACE questions are as follows:

T - Does it **take** more than three drinks to make you feel high?

A - Have you ever been **annoyed** by people's criticism of your drinking?

C - Are you trying to **cut down** on drinking?

E - Have you ever used alcohol as an **eye opener** in the morning?

Again, "yes" answers to two of these four questions is an indication of possible alcohol abuse or dependence. This test is a better indicator that you may already be an alcoholic or you are well started on that course. If 2 or more answers are positive, then, again, seek professional testing from a local substance abuse Counsellor.

The AUDIT Test

The Counsellor might administer one of the most accurate tests available, which is the Alcohol Use Disorders Identification Test (AUDIT). This test has been rated as being accurate 94 percent of the time. It is also accurate across ethnic and gender groups, so it eliminates the biases of shorter screening questionnaires. The test contains 10 multiple choice questions that are scored on a point system. A score of more than eight indicates an alcohol problem.

The disadvantage of the AUDIT test, developed by the World Health Organization, is that it takes longer to administer and, compared to the shorter tests, it is more difficult to score. Frankly, this is a pretty minor disadvantage: an experienced Counsellor can administer the AUDIT and give you a score within an hour or two—and counsel you to follow a particular treatment course.

About the Author

Richard Thatcher is a clinical sociologist, social worker and social planning consultant who has worked for several decades in both social and health service fields. As a Counsellor he has focused a good deal of his attention on substance abuse and behavioural dependencies. Much of his work has been with indigenous North American communities and organizations.*

The author of three books, including *Vision Seekers: A Structured Personal and Social Development Program for First Nations' youth at High Social Risk* (2001); *Deadly Duo: Tobacco and Convenience Foods—The Other Substance Abuse Epidemics Afflicting the First Nations and Inuit of Canada* (2001); and *Fighting Firewater Fictions: Beyond the Disease Model of Addictions in First Nations* (2004), Dr. Thatcher has also prepared hundreds of technical studies of local, regional and national scope for governments and non-profit organizations, including program evaluations and designs for substance abuse treatment centres for youth.

Dr. Thatcher has a Ph.D., M.A. and B.A. He is a licensed professional social worker in private practice and a certified clinical sociologist. He is now semi-retired and lives with his wife in a converted school house in the rural village of Craven, just twenty minutes from Regina, the capital city of the Canadian province of Saskatchewan.

---

* Referred to as "peoples of the First Nations" in Canada and as "Native Americans" in the United States.